JUST BE:

My Healing Journey to Embrace the Mess

Written by
Liz Kametz

Just Be Publishing
Glastonbury, CT USA

Cover credit: Mik Advertising & Design, LLC.
Back cover: Mik Advertising & Design, LLC.

ISBN-13: 978-1-7357166-0-2
Library of Congress Control Number: 2020917093

www.justbethejourney.com
Email: info@justbethejourney.com

DEDICATION

To Each of You. Love Yourself.

Content

"Everything in my life works now
and forevermore."

—Louise Hay

Introduction

Waking up

Do you remember that feeling when you were a kid, at an age when sleep seemed to only come right at the moment everyone else wanted you awake—and your mom or dad, or even just the alarm clock, was right there waking you up? It felt jarring. Your body shook and you squirmed away under the covers with barely an audible groan to resist, asking *Why do I HAVE to wake up now?*

Your soul's awakening is just like that, or any major life-changing moment that comes into your life. It's not fun. When it happens, you kind of just want to squirm under the covers, lift them over your head, and go back to sleep. You didn't ASK for this, did you? Or maybe you did, a silent prayer under your breath asking for change. Others might be numb to the itch, the need to change. Whatever place you're in when the awakening comes it's shocking—for your mind, body and soul. It's an active, sometimes violent, experience, that often comes through stillness.

That's the type of contradiction it presents: action through stillness; calm through chaos; all the while opening and expanding your personal self-knowing.

I've spent a lot of time studying my life and my experiences. I don't have a degree to do this, just a yearning to excavate, uncover, brush off and admire my findings. I'm hoping that through my own archeological dig of myself, others can start, continue or expand their own self-discovery.

All I have is my experience to give and I'm hopeful that my storytelling shines light on each of you who take the time to listen, to my story, to your own, and especially to the youthful part of you that might be screaming to be heard like mine was.

Excerpts from this book have been woven together from years of journaling, but the impetus to spend the time to lace it all together came from the collective 'awakening' we are experiencing with COVID-19. Although pockets of champions of self-care have been around for many years, the collective calling to slow down, go back to basics, get re-grounded in your beliefs, seemed to me, to skyrocket when the pandemic took over our lives.

The time is right to keep open minds, body and soul on the importance of self-love, authenticity and true connection. The question is: how do we look within and truly honor ourselves, completely?

That's the part I am unwilling to forget since I woke up.

Getting Started on Your Just-Be Path

Here's what you need to know before we get started:

- I've written these excerpts spanning over the last 5 years.
- I've experienced a *great* childhood with a conventional family unit of mom, dad, and older brother.
- I've experienced the 'new' conventional family unit of mom, stepdad, dad, stepmom, and older brother.
- I set and achieved goals of the highest level of education, marriage, children and positive career.
- I'm a mom of two boys with special needs, who teach me more in a day than I've learned in any school.
- I was married, then divorced, now married again—I believe in the convention of marriage and always believe in LOVE.
- I've traveled the world.
- I'm like you in many ways, unique in others, and this book that binds us invisibly together is that of both seeker and learner together.
- I have a deep desire to learn and grow, trying to do good for myself and others.

Before you take this journey with me, I need you to remember to 'just-be' YOU—that's the journey. I'll be doing the same thing too. With you, I will share pieces of my life and journey, and guess what? It's not linear, because nothing in life is. It jumps and winds around in spirals—exactly as it should.

I encourage you to keep your own journal. As you read my journey, reflect on your own. What emotions, reflections, desires, do my stories invoke in you? Write what you felt as you're reading each vignette. Which vignettes can you relate to? Reflect on the affirmations. This will come in handy at the end of each section of this book. Let this book be another tool to help you look within and truly honor yourself, completely. At least, that's what writing it has demanded: I don't forget for myself.

Liz Kametz - Midsummer, 2020

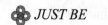

Turning Pages

There I am, a child, right before my third birthday. Silent and peaceful. Love all around me. I adore my older brother, feeling protected, being loved. *Turn the page.*

Woken by noise. Maybe a stomach ache. Maybe it was only nerves. I run downstairs to the light of the family room, seeking comfort in my mother's embrace. *What did I find?* A scene too much—too heavy—to share with the world, to this day my inner child is still too afraid. *Turn the page.*

There I am, a little bit older, observing the world around me, yet living completely inside. Inside my thoughts. Inside my imagination, still content, but maybe already contained.
Turn the page.

Now age seven. My mother is no longer at home—gone to work—when my whole life has been *her* being there all the time. A male babysitter is watching us, making me uncomfortable and frightened again. He tells me I'm so pretty, but it makes me feel wrong and not pretty at all.

Waiting on the front step for my mother to save me. When she does come home, she dismisses my world. Claims I exaggerated, that of course *I'm so beautiful*, and of course he would say so. More containers are built, how I should feel, how I should be.
Turn the page.

Now a young teenager, wise beyond years, knowing exactly the 'shoulds' that people expect from me. Seeking the love and protection, that I knew was there when I was just three. Finding solace in friends and boyfriends, to mimic the life I thought I should have. Using my body, to gain the attention, my inner child, so desperate.
Turn the page.

Parents' divorce. Admit they 'knew' for seven years but wanted to raise us together, as loving parents. All four of us hug and cry in the family room where so much has happened. Where many concrete walls have risen, in my inner world, to protect me, to protect the existence I thought I should have.
Turn the page.

Goals were set. Life moves forward: checking the boxes, maintaining the love, through pleasing and acquiescing, to the world of expectations all around.
Turn the page.

Married with child. Love became known and for the first time is real. My son is my *true* love. My husband leaves me stranded, a jealous bystander, not knowing how to be. His hurt guided him to another, then boomeranged into our world. While my broken heart and shattered dreams led me on a path toward my own healing. My own awakening begins. *Turn the page.*

Forgiveness amongst us. Second chances abound and very hopeful that what *should be*, could still be found. Another son granted. This one also an angel showing what pure joy and peace can look like, unabridged. *Turn the page.*

Dark shadows cast upon the hopes and dreams, as troubles stir with the rising of children's special needs. One with autism. The other soon-to-be broken. Husband left. Only their Dad in name... and darkness grew heavy with each living breath. *Turn the page.*

The strength of my connections, the strongest women united, to share their light and lift my load. Deep self-reflection, awareness created, and the recognition of the path my inner child was on. Looking back to learn, to reach for that girl, who started to build containers and walls so long ago. *Turn the page.*

Demolition is among us. The sledgehammer is out. I stand strong by the side of my little Liz ready to tear down all the walls of *shoulds* that were built. Love has been found again, with a new hubby and children: a new family to forge, with its own difficult paths. *Turn the page...*

Affirmation: *Today, I will turn the page on an old chapter in my life.*

Achiever, Pleaser, Pumpkin Eater

I always remember the feeling of being teased. The singsong effect the bullies had if they were smart, created a twisted feeling of shame and jealousy while it was happening. I wanted to be one of them, but some part of me knew that wanting to be someone who made someone else feel bad was not a good goal to strive for. So maybe it was just to avoid having to be the one being made fun of—*do it or it will be done to you.*

Perfectionism was my poison. It was a dish I was fed at a very early age, and unbeknownst to me, was highly toxic. I was a happy girl—happy teen, happy college girl—for the most part. I was able to succeed at anything I set out to do; I just made sure I knew I could do it before I even started. Anything 'tough' or 'not natural,' I didn't try, because I was told I had so many natural gifts that would give me success: dancing, singing, math, science, communicating, relationships, beauty.

I was a natural at a lot, so it never felt hard to be 'perfect.'

I wasn't raised understanding what 'struggle' or 'hard' really meant, until the day I found out my husband was having an affair. In hindsight, it's like I lived a life blinded to the beauty of pain and loss, not to mention struggle for thirty years.

What I didn't realize (because I was living without my eyes really open) was that 'pain' and 'hard' had knocked on my door already—every day, maybe. But there was no room for that I'm the perfect world I was expected to live. I learned, instinctively, to cast it deep inside.

In my own individual excavation, I've come to learn a light will ignite in your own self-exploration and growth with a little peace of mind that as unique as we are, we are connected through moments, trying and joyful, that weave our humanity together.

Affirmation: *I ignite the light inside me for my own exploration, bringing to my life peace of mind.*

The Day the Music Died

I grew up with the perfect picture of what life should be as an adult. It included all the Disney fed imagery of Prince Charming, with a splattering of *Cosby Show, Family Ties* and *Growing Pains*. I would watch the '80s sitcoms after school and my subconscious constructed my expectations for my future, unknowingly.

As a very goal-oriented girl, who was always told I could do anything I wanted to, I had 100% certainty that this future picture would become real. That I had the power to make it so. I was so sucked into becoming a wife and mother and creating a fantasy family unit, like on TV, I was blind to reality. My constructs (my music), built up over time, created the filter through which I saw life unfold.

My music died the day my phone rang early, one morning, an average day. The baby was still sleeping and I'd started the day's work. Something told me intuitively that this call meant *danger*, a warning, even before I picked up the phone. My body kicked my heart rate into gear and made my stomach queasy. My mind, in its make-believe fantasy, had a tougher time catching up—*Who would be calling this early?*

I picked up the phone, heard a man introduce himself as the husband of the woman with whom *my* husband was having an affair. In that moment, my beautiful music that had been playing inside me—since childhood—went silent. It's been twelve years since and I'm still not sure I've let another song in. The silence has been many things: deafening, peaceful, lonely, maddening, confusing, scary, hard to trust and inspirational.

I've learned that setting goals is different than living in a predetermined frame I *should* be living; having a dream won't kill you, if it doesn't come true, but not being open to the flow of what truly is, might.

In a way, I've been searching for my new music ever since that day, but haven't trusted letting it in. I'm realizing that feeling lost with no purpose is just my mind's way of trying to understand where the music went.

The amazing thing is that I've stopped searching for it. I let go and tried to just be. When that happened, I heard the faint sound of my own soul's music that was always there, waiting for me to come home.

Affirmation: *I let go of searching, and hear the sound of my own soul's music.*

Anxiety

Feeling very unsettled about leaving my boys this week. I think it's because they have school and I can't be in control of what they eat, how they sleep, and so on. Plus, I feel like even if something goes wrong, I can't be here to help. It's hard to trust others in these situations.

My anxiety is rising, so I feel like that means the boys' anxiety will be too…

Plus, there is so much to juggle to get things straight before we leave, and with the housework going on, it's overwhelming.

Lots of lack of control moments all layered on top of each other.

Breathe.

Affirmation: *Today, I will breathe through the difficult moments and trust myself.*

Generations

As I try to listen, learn and reflect from those of multiple generations, one of the main themes I hear parents talk about is giving or doing better than what they had. For most, it seems this might come in the form of having more *things*, like a car or vacations. Or it could mean more opportunities, like going further in school, and even still, it could mean simply projecting what success looks like—being a doctor or a lawyer is better than a blue-collar worker—also known as making more money equals a better life.

I'm struggling with this concept for my children.

It's like when adults say, "He knew what he was doing and that it was wrong," or "He was doing this for no apparent reason, there's no excuse." Even when things like this are said, it's usually when it has been awhile since my son has shown aggressive behavior, and it'd be more appropriate to ask, "What's happening with him that could have triggered this behavior?" -- But they don't.

I find myself wanting *better* in a way that is much more simplistic— better emotional stability; better intrinsic happiness seeking—Perhaps we each define our version of *better* based on the struggles we've had in our past and based on the way we were taught generationally. I know my struggles are those of emotional neglect—so my version of *better* is the desire for more emotional inclusion for my children.

Affirmation: *I honor all who have come before and soak in the learnings from the generations.*

What Does the Universe Say?

This whole week I've been feeling on edge, but not certain why. It must be trepidation for a new change with my job, but there isn't really anything to think about or do except wait. I'll get waves of unease and anxiety with no thoughts associated to it, only the feeling of butterflies in my stomach and my heart racing. I try to avoid the feeling by thinking of things to do, being productive, checking things off the list. But I know that I'm supposed to just be still and lean in… and breathe…

I've also been worrying more about my youngest lately. He's my boy who is so sensitive to others and wants to be loved, accepted, wanted. And when those things don't feel right for him, he takes it out on the world through anger and sadness. He is not my talker; he's my doer. I have a tough time connecting, since I'm such a talker. I want to be there for him. I want him to know I'm always there for him, that I'm always here to give love and support.

And I want him to HEAR those words. Spending time with him does communicate that to him, without the words themselves, though it seems foreign to me.

Today we finished his last Occupational Therapy session. On the way home, I suggested asking his friend up the street to play. He went to the door and said, "Want to play?" No one did. My son got upset, believing his friend was upset with him. I explained it probably had nothing to do with him, that people carry their emotions from other experiences throughout the day. As a mom, I just see my sad baby getting rejected and someone slamming the door. How do I help show him it's okay to be upset, and let out that emotion, and not to pass it on? Not in violence or through revenge?

Another time, I let the boys stay home alone for an hour, here and there, and although, it seems appropriate in some ways, it triggers my own past of not wanting to be left alone at that age, abandoned. With the trigger comes really uncomfortable feelings boiling below the surface like self-contempt and self-criticism. Yesterday I let them stay home and made the decision the kids were fine and I could enjoy a night out. Nothing happened to the boys, but I felt like a failure and ended up having anger toward myself.

My internal shame script says:

Why are you putting yourself before your children? Who gives you the right to have fun while you abandon the kids at home? Pull yourself together, you are not being the best mom you are supposed to be. You are failing them; you are failing me.

I remember feeling like this the first time I left my kids with someone else. No one could be good enough for them except me.

The crux of it is acknowledging I lived in constant fear, carried from my little self, who didn't want to be left alone. Then as I moved through life, I was reinforced that *if* left alone, bad things would happen. Nothing really bad happened except my oldest telling me he was sad I wasn't home quick enough. Ironically though, my body today has been reliving the shame and agony and ultimately, the rooted fear I've carried for almost my whole life.

I've gotten my mind, body and soul to agree that taking care of myself is absolutely necessary to be the best mom I can be. It doesn't mean guilt doesn't show up from time to time.

How do I define self-care? It takes time to move from what seems reckless to recognizing it could just be fun. It's redeciding where my core values actually fall and reflecting back, *would I do it again?* And allowing the decision to come not from guilt, fear, or shame, but somewhere else. Some days, I've got it. Other days, my body is screaming for me to pay attention.

So, I write, then pause, and see what the universe says.

Affirmation: *I am not my thoughts. I will let them flow. Always present, trusting the universe.*

Spiritual Divorce

In a book exploring spiritual divorce, the author writes, "This book is about healing the biggest hurt that life can inflict: the ending of a dream, the loss of a love, (See: *Divorce as a Catalyst for an Extraordinary Life, Spiritual Divorce,* Debbie Ford, Copyright 2001).

I break down sobbing.

That's what it is then, that's what's happened, from birth to age thirty-three, I literally was living a dream. And it felt really good, of course—I'm sure there were times it didn't—but somehow, I just kept sleeping. I didn't actually wake up and join reality, until I was pushed out of my dream by my then husband.

And reality sucks.

If you knew me you might think I'm the last person to follow that gimmicky statement, reality sucks! But I went along life thinking *reality* is good, so long as you keep making it good. Just think positive and all will be positive. Somehow when I woke up from my 'dream' those beliefs didn't come to reality with me. They are lost in my dreamland. I can sense them, but they are too far removed from *the me* I am every day. I want to go back to sleep—ironically, since the divorce, sleep is something I have lost as well...

My mind starts to think of all the references of books/movies that this theme plays out. The 1998 film, *City of Angels* comes to mind. Nicholas Cage *literally* falls from the heavens and feels pain for the first time. I'm not trying to equate myself to an angel, but don't we all have some angelic qualities. Especially as children, before we are biased by all the experiences life throws. In the classic 1990s sci-fi movie, *The Matrix,* the world we live in is just a dream. For Keanu Reeves, waking up physically hurt!

So what's the message?

On one side, I'm regretful that I had to wait this long to wake up. What did I miss by holding on to my dream for so long? On the other side, I'm angry—so angry—because (*what-the-F)* now I have to deal with all this pain when I KNOW how good the dream felt!

A therapist might say it all goes back to how we are raised and formed. What if I'm catching up from what I missed the first thirty years? How long do I have to drink this up and learn from this? Will it ever go away, enough that it doesn't always feel like I'm drowning? When will I get to float on the water and soak up the sun again and actually rejoice in the coolness the water provides?

Here's the thing. Entering into reality from a dream is like re-learning life. Go with me on this: year one of divorce—totally grief cycle, survival mode. Year two—self-reflection, healing. Year three, four, five—hope, but mixed in with a LOT of pain. After that, there is a lot of pain. You fall a lot. The real kicker? I'm doing it alone!

There isn't a mom or dad or any other family there to hold your hand during your first steps. You have to take them *by yourself.* What person in their right mind would do this? Why not just sit back down and go back to the dream?

I keep using the term pain, and by this I just mean struggle. For me pain is seeing someone I love angry, or sad or frustrated or mean, or, or, or, ...fill in the negative word and there you have it.

Pain for me is having to live through all those negative emotions that I'm ill-equipped to handle. But I'm learning. I CAN do this alone, and with the support of my people. One day soon I might be able to smile at someone else's pain and say, "I see you and it's going to be okay."

Affirmation: *I close my eyes, breathe deep, and let what rises be acknowledged.*

Through Thick and Thin

I remember when my then-husband took me and my son to a work picnic only weeks after learning that he had started an affair with a woman at his job. Why did I go? Why did I let him walk all over my heart? He had us drive to his work first, which I had found out was the area he had started his affair. After, we drove to the picnic where she would be.

My body was screaming at me, through white knuckles clenching, heart racing, and nervous system going completely haywire. All those signals, I didn't listen. I kept going. I held my head up, grasped my son for dear life, and moved like I was mud, as time passed by. One breath at a time. One heartbeat after the other. Is this true survival, the persistence to continue? Is this the meaning of the phrase, *through thick or thin*? The times in life when just moving from one minute to the next feels like the weight of the world but we do it anyway?

Something I was watching, recently, brought me back to that day and made me feel regret.

Remorse for not standing up for myself, or giving myself the right to be mad, sad, or stationary even—not trying so hard to *just keep going*. It's like those in-between-times, when you finally pause between moments and let yourself get still. Those are the moments that are actually the scariest. Perhaps when we are truly operating in survival, there is no way our instincts will let us have that pause, because it could mean too much risk. (In the animal world, it could be the difference of life or death).

I gave myself that ultimate pause seven years later—and what an awakening!

And since all the time that has passed, being transported back to that day and conjuring up feelings of regret and remorse can only mean I better pay attention next time things feel *thick.*

It's time to recognize I *am* powerful enough to get through the thickness, to remind my inner wounded-self it's time to allow for the space to be still. And there's no need to wait seven years. Just let it flow.

Affirmation: *Today I take back my power, own my strength and rejoice.*

Life Choices Are a Rubik's Cube

So we start off and follow our guides, our parents, teachers, trusted supporters to help us in the types of decisions we make and how to keep our life in balance (e.g., solid colors on each side of the cube, the starting point) and then life meanders and choices are sometimes made for us, circumstances thrust at us, and before we know it, we have a scrambled Rubik's Cube where no like-color touches another. This feels very jarring and uncomfortable for those of us who like order and control. We like to color inside the lines and appreciate a good rainbow as long as the order is the way we expect it to be. So here we are, struggling to shift moments, movement by movement to get our alignment back, 'solve' the puzzle.

But I've realized something. I'm not sure the effort, frustration, hopelessness and overall stress it creates to try and get back to where we started is worth it. I think we could just put the cube down, and grab a new one.

Or—even tougher, accept the cube with all its variations and relish in the uniqueness that each new moment, each decision creates for ourselves. I'm going to try that.

Next time my kids are testing my limits of patience, I'm going to picture my Rubik's Cube of scattered disarrayed colors and honor the complex, rich, beauty it is without judgment, criticism or attempt to 'put it back' the way it's 'supposed' to be. Might you join me to try that as well with your own Rubik's Cube of life?

Affirmation: *All is as it is meant to be.*

Missing Moments

I saw a picture of my boys when they were younger and didn't recognize my youngest at all.

How could I not recognize my own son?

It's not like I was working so many hours a week and barely with them; I was with them **all the time**.

The picture mystified me. Then something clicked: *how much time do we live in survival mode and not really open our eyes each day to the present moment?*

My older son looked relatively the same. But with my youngest, the photo captured a short-lived trend that passed quickly. Without the photo, it would've been lost forever. How did I allow my circumstances of divorce to cost me this phase of my son's life?

Some days, I miss the time when I could carry the kids around on my hip, when they were still growing in those years, which have now passed. It feels like the divorce took those tangible moments from me. I'll never get that time back. I'll never be able to carry my babies in my arms again. And some days that makes me angry at myself, my ex-husband, the world.

My favorite childhood memories do not include my mom carrying me around on her hip. But when I look at the pictures of the boys, I can't help but miss the safety and security I felt when I was providing it, and swung them up on my hip like it was nothing. That feeling of the child's whole body holding onto yours with dear life, is a representation of them saying, "Mom, you better not let go, because I have no clue what's under me, or in front of me, or if I can even walk further, or get through it. You

31

better hold onto me, okay?" Meanwhile, the mom is thinking, "Okay, how do I keep hold of this kid, and my purse, and the grocery bag, while trying to open my locked doors?"

Yes, that feeling! You can't get it back. It's so fragile, so quick, that it becomes a memory in an instant.

Maybe I can look towards being a grandma to get it back! ☺

Affirmation: *I reflect on moments I might have missed and give space to the feelings that come.*

We Teach Best What We Have to Learn

Sometimes I get worried that negativity is overcoming our household. I've been trying to live up to my beliefs of love and compassion leading us, but when my youngest can't deal with the outburst of the kids around him, I want to throw my hands up and give in to the evil.

Before dinner, I speak to him calmly, affirming everything will be all right. But like most of us, he feels it will be like this tomorrow. How can I fault him? I still have yet to embrace the truth that negativity is not the enemy; it's not the evil. All emotions are just channels of communication to listen.

How can I help him let go and focus on today?

Bad behavior is just a child's way to communicate that something is wrong.

We teach best what we have to learn.

Affirmation: *I observe my family's behaviors and view it as messages to listen.*

Warning: Process This Slow

These past few weeks have been tough. It's like I'm stuck inside the depression game. I changed jobs in hopes to pursue some independent feelings of value and success, but it turns out it's just feeding into the stress and negativity the rest of my life seems to bear.

I find myself reflecting on my parents' divorce and the process by which we were told and experienced it. Even though it was over twenty-five years ago, I feel like many of my behaviors and reactions to current life are because of the lack of healing I've really been able to do on behalf of the fifteen-year-old girl who lived through it. Because everything was hidden, and all the change/transition happened to blind eyes, it felt like the day they told us they were divorcing happened in the flick of a switch.

One day we were a solid family unit and the next, a whole new world began. My father drove us to his new house, which was all set up with things from our old house, plus new stuff too. The drastic flip somehow cast a feeling of 'it's not okay to process this slow.' I never feared my parents didn't love me, and of course, I was a teenager, so in essence self-absorbed and compartmentalized to keep life going.

How does that help me with the present? I jot down the following: I'm worried about the stress of all my family members right now and I find myself hyper-sensitive and overreacting to everything.

Inner voice: Well, this isn't yours to fix, even if it is a problem.
But I do need to know how to 'fix' my reaction to it. I feel poisoned...

Inner voice: Can you explain what you mean by poisoned?

It feels like a virus of negativity takes over very quickly. I'm actually depressed again. My stomach hurts and I'm chewing off everyone's head.

Inner voice: What's your fear?

It's weird, sometimes, when I can't remember feeling scared or worried at certain times in my life. Why is that? I can transport myself back to it very easily, but can't feel the emotion.

Inner voice: You repressed it.

Loss of control. Fear of unknown and raw emotions I didn't want to face—maybe it was the little self, afraid of all the things I was afraid of as a kid that made it impossible to process the changes slow. I can generally figure that any intense emotion that seems out of proportion to the actual situation is probably coming from that little girl.

Today, I talk to her and comfort her, letting her know everything is safe and going slow is okay.

Affirmation: *Today, I let my little self know everything is safe and going slow is okay.*

Family Mosaic

Part of what I struggle with when I read about others journeying towards their light is the fact that their family is intact. This doesn't mean there aren't struggles in the marriage or how difficult the children are to parent, but there is this concept of a complete entity, wholeness. The minute divorce strikes, the wholeness is broken, shattered into thousands of pieces.

As the child of divorce, I know how this feels, but as the parent and ex-wife of divorce, it's even harder. It feels like I'm spending the rest of life putting back the pieces. And in that mosaic can come a beauty that could have never been realized. I still struggle with comparing my mosaic plate of life to the one that is whole. Perhaps others have scratches or even missing pieces that can feel equally painful, but I'm stuck comparing my mosaic just wishing to be whole.

That's the problem with comparisons. One person feels less because of money, or fame, or material things, or relationships. And I feel less because I don't have the family it seems many have. That only leaves me with feeling less, and although I want to have/need less, I want to *feel* more, allow all my feelings to flow through. Say hello, offer tea, and let them go.

I'm considering the benefits of allowing space, slowing down, and asking for help, and saying 'no' as a form of self-care, and through all of it, I nod in recognition. 'I'm doing this,' I say to myself, 'I've learned this already.' But still, I'm left comparing. This is great, but she doesn't know what's it's like to be a single mom or she doesn't know what it's like to support a blended family, or she doesn't know what it's like to raise special needs children. But where does this comparison leave me? Not isolated, acting like a victim? Or is it? Why is it so hard for me to stay open, honor someone else's struggle even though it's not the same as mine, to learn from them anyway? Why can't it just be the truth that we *all struggle* that can connect us? No matter the size, or look or scariness of each individual's monster they are wrestling, we are connected in the struggle itself.

The land of comparison seems very congested, there is no peace here. Only noise, bumping into each other, crime, jealousy, hatred, competition, darkness and in my imagination, there is no place for a flower or a tree to grow. If there is no place for nature, why do I stay? How can I get out of this land? Some say through gratitude and positive affirmations, we will move away from this land. Others say, *just look at how much you have compared to the hungry or homeless!* as if a victim themselves, not being able to dream beyond their ancestors or the homeless.

Awareness seems to always be the first step. That and breathing. In with the land of comparison, without resistance.

I'll just walk through and continue on to the light that calls me.

Affirmation: *My family mosaic is as unique as a snowflake. I take wonder in its beauty.*

Emotional Cinderella

Do you ever have one emotion trigger and then another? There have been multiple times in my life when I have felt my entire body wash over me with love and peace and in that instant, that very instant, I begin to cry. Not the joyous cry you have during a wedding, or the joyous cry you have with friends, but the sorrowful cry, the mournful cry.

It happens when I hear news about my ex-husband making a move and taking an interest in being a parent again, enough to think, he might finally be opening his eyes to what life is really about. It's been seven years, and still, I sob over the loss I feel... I sob over the idea of what those years could have been like *with* him and what I believed a family should look like... that his choices changed.

It's like I grew up with the crystal palace (now realizing this is probably very seeded in Disney and Cinderella and isn't that crazy how much influence that had on my perception of what a 'dream' life would be?) that was just perfect. The glass palace where everything had its place, where love was the only thing present, where I was the 'perfect little girl' and there was no conscious fear that I couldn't live up to that label. It took my divorce to truly have that castle fall to shambles. In retrospect, I never noticed the glass shattering with my parents' divorce because the love inside was too strong, which I guess is a good thing. I was still blind and deaf to the shattering of that glass.

But the glass shattering from my divorce cut through me; I was brought to my hands and knees, or more literally, a fetal position in my son's toddler bed on the first nights when they weren't in my home. I remember thinking, this is not natural. This is not the way nature intended, a child should not be sleeping without his mother by his side. My then husband's choices changed that. And as a result, it 'broke' my version of what life should be, the natural order.

And now, seven years later he is coming back… not to me, but back to the idea of what a parent should be. Somehow his growth is breaking me again, or I'm allowing it to. Somehow his recognition of what 'should' be, is reopening old wounds. Instead of thinking about how good this will be for the boys, I feel the loss and mourning again of what could have been.

Maybe today was an emotional one without me even knowing it. It brings change, which I know firsthand means I will journey through the change curve. My outburst of emotion is linked to the stage of sadness I need to move through about the change.

Affirmation: *The loss cycle is real and slow. I am okay with its pace and stay open to what there is to learn.*

Weightlessness

Parenting is inconvenient, but because you never want to be inconvenienced, and the priority is never what you need, but what the kids do, I'm left with the burden of inconvenience all the time.

I'm back on the island of misfit toys, with my boys, and it appears I'm the only one that can live with them, and sometimes I feel like I even can't. (There I admitted it).

I guess I'm getting used to being a nag.

I have this emptiness inside. How could I miss my kids when I spent the entire weekend frustrated at their lack of listening, lack of compassion, constant fighting and me trying to referee? Then, when I'm around it, all I can think is 'get me out of here!' But then when I have space without it, I feel wrong, vacant, like something is missing.

Do I really miss being a nag?

As a divorced parent it feels like it's either carrying *all* the weight, or nothing at all when they are gone. My kids come with a heavy weight; they come with stubbornness, rigidity, inattention, hyperactivity, trauma, grief, anxiety, anger, pain, and they lay it out all right there in front of you. I've always felt like I have to lighten that load for them, carry some for them and teach them how to let go. But the weight is so heavy. Then it's gone, just like that.

I'm not a bodybuilder—the furthest thing from it—but I have experienced that feeling when you lift something heavy and put your muscles to their limit and then let go—how conversely light it feels, untethered and birdlike. But with that drastic change in life, I'm afraid I'll float away, the lightness is almost unnerving.

Weightlessness leaves me without any sense of being grounded. Their weight grounds me. But then it nails me down and suffocates me too and I start kicking and screaming for air. The imbalance is not healthy; it's the true source of discomfort, not weight or flight, but the drastic distance between the two.

Can a normal balance be achieved with just one parent—or does it take more of something to distribute the weight?

I know that my best self is one who stands by my little ones, as they hang heavy. I stay with them, honoring their pain. I know this, but have not learned how to let go.

The key is being able to do both.

Affirmation: *I place bare feet to the earth, welcoming its strength to keep me grounded.*

Nothing to Fix

If you have experienced any child with enhanced needs (that's what they're calling it now), you'll know that when things are *off*, they're OFF and EVERYTHING is hard.

"Get your shoes on."

"Get in the car."

"Brush your teeth."

"Pick up that cup you just threw on the floor."

"Stop chewing the wire."

"Stop chewing your fingers."

"Stop making noises."

"Stop antagonizing your brother."

"What is the matter?"

"What's wrong with you?"

"Why do you have to be so difficult?"

He spits.

I slap.

He flips my chair upside down while I'm sitting in it.

He runs out.

I run out.

Both fuming, getting in the car.

The younger one along for the ride—not the fun kind, but the scary, pitch-black rollercoaster from hell that no one asked for.

The older one says, "You shouldn't slap me! I should tell the cops."

"Good idea, let's go to the station!"

I drive to the station.

Park the car.

"Get out of the car!"

The younger one is crying, "Mommy, please, I'm scared."

My heart is broken. I already know there's no good in these moments.

The older one gets back in the car.

Drive home in silence. Part of me thinks, *really?* This is what it takes to get the quiet I need?

My actions are unjust.

My finger is pointed right back at me.

I stew, and then try to breathe.

I wait. I remove myself.

Today is a hard day.

No fixing can happen. Just rest.

These types of days are frequent in times of major change or high stress, of which we have both.

My son has always been inquisitive beyond his years, but now, into his adolescence, his questions are spot on—

"Can someone learn how to be less impulsive?"

"How about controlling their anger?"

I tell him it helps to have time for self-care, to do what you love, connect with friends, get rest, recharge.

And he says, "You should do that then Mom."

Affirmation: *Children are our guides to learn, please grace me the space to receive.*

What is Normal

I remember the first time I caught myself saying my son was *not normal,* that he was on the *spectrum.*

But what is normal?

This 2020 quarantine has forced us to put the word *normal* under the magnifying glass.

In 1743 it was *normal* to cut a hand off for stealing.

In Japan it's *normal* to bathe in hot springs naked with strangers without judgment or shame.

In our current time and place, it's *normal* to expect our children to play multiple sports, maybe an instrument, think about what occupation they will pursue, participate in social connections, seamlessly, and get good grades.

I try like hell to remove judgment from my being, but I can't help but judge each and every *normal* I just outlined.

Now our *normal* is being home **A LOT**, wearing masks in public, worrying about spreading a virus, and worrying if our kids will get the carefree childhood they deserve. Again, the idea of *normal* should probably be destroyed. Perhaps if we didn't grant any attention to *normal* and just allowed what IS, we would have an easier time riding the constant wave of change that is our current world.

Be it a *typical* student versus *special ed.*

Normal life versus *alternative.*

I beg of us, let's remove the *italics* and Just Be.

Affirmation: *I relinquish all expectations.*

Measuring Love

I've come to realize that the amount of love someone has been given as a child has a lot to do with the way they live their life as an adult.

How do you measure love?

Am I the sole provider of love for my children?

My inner voice replies: Your job is opening doors; you can't hold their hand and walk through each door with each person you love dearly.

They will walk alone or find someone to hold their hand, but it doesn't have to be you.

Just keep shining the light on the doors.

You are the gatekeeper; they hold the key. As do you with your journey.

Affirmation: *I sit in the light of my own love and trust its infinite ability to spread.*

Creating Fear

Today, I took my boys to the trampoline park. It's become a good go-to spot where they burn off some energy, exercise, and generally feel good about themselves. Lately, my oldest has wanted to land a backflip and is too scared to do so. He blames his fear on me.

He says to me, "If you hadn't drilled it in me to be scared that I might land on my head and become paralyzed or die then I wouldn't be so afraid!"

I explain I'd said it because I didn't want to risk him trying something he wasn't ready for.

"Well, Mom, it would have been *way* more effective if you had just said to me, 'you're not capable yet. So please don't try, as soon as we think you're ready and have practiced enough you can try,' this way, I wouldn't have fear to carry with me.

Hmm, in retrospect, I guess we all can learn a bit about parenting at any age.

Maybe all my failed attempts at the right parenting methods are just arming my kids to be even better. Instead of worrying so much about if I'm going to fail, I could be reinforcing when I do, so we can all learn at the same time.

"You're right," I told him. "It would have been a much better way to prepare you."

And the wheel just keeps turning round and round, learning from each other every day.

Affirmation: *I believe failure is one of the best ways to learn and grow.*

47

Fight, Flight, or Freeze

Fear can trigger three different reactions: fight, flight, or freeze. I've had moments in my life that have felt frozen from two days to two years. It's being immobilized and trying to decide what to do next. What foot to put forward and to go where.

Times like this, I'm living from—or maybe in—my head. It takes time to become friends with my thoughts. I watch how they take me down the *'what if?'* highway, Sometimes I ride along, watching, from a distance.

Distance is good when things are unclear. It gives me time to work through my instincts, which often tell me the threat has not gone away yet.

Today, when tensions rose in a household full of judgment and shame, I watched as my kids took flight to their rooms, to the furthest corners of the house.

Escape is a means to wait out the storm. As the rain is pouring, thunder roaring, we hunker down and wait, escaping the pounding of the rain's criticism on our back.

The rain stops.

Is it safe to come out?

Like the Munchkins of Munchkin Land in Oz, you might need your fairy godmother to tell you it's okay to 'come out, come out, wherever you are.' So my son peeks his head around a door, with a demanding call of "Mom!?!" I am his fairy godmother helping him assess if it's safe to come out.

Has the storm passed? Will I be safe from the shame rain?

Today, I tried not to get trapped in the storm. I tried to put my gear on, become a meteorologist for my son, and for my little self, and not completely escape, just recede, to allow the space of judgment to breathe.

Hoping the space would eventually starve the judgment, as it needs action and debate to fuel its engine.
Now the storm has passed, but do any of us feel safe to come out? It's up to me to encourage my little self and my son that they are never alone, I am here, keeping watch, to hold them tight so the need for fight, flight, or freeze will be honored from a distance.

Affirmation: *I brave the balance of human instinct with life experience to guide me.*

Healing

I put so much on my kids' behavior being my fault. It's societal, maybe, even if I remind myself that there are things not in my control. Still, when things go wrong, I feel the judgment and just continue to make that judgment my own.

You know that lump in the throat that comes so suddenly when sadness hits without warning? It happens sometimes when I remember things said to me like, "I just don't love you anymore, but I don't know why."

I've spent many years moving through my grief of the loss of my marriage, trying to make sure I didn't avoid the process, but experienced *each* stage that was needed for *true* healing. But just when I seem close to healing that wound, I get a lump in the throat; my body and mind play catch up as I catch myself with the fleeting thoughts of *what if it didn't happen? What if we were able to make things work and we were still a family unit?*

The truth is that the body knows it's still mourning. I have yet to truly let go, the original trauma of my childhood family unit shattering—the first that never healed, and without any warning, realizing how my traumas are linked, and thus, create a deeper wound to heal, with frequent triggers to navigate, toward healing.

My body still catches me with silly lumps in the throat, tears in the eyes, and tightness in the chest—all signs my little child inside is still aching for those shattered pieces to be put back together again.

Why can't all the king's horses and all the king's men put Humpty back together again? Is that one of those twisted nursery rhymes that really just implies, *'Well, kid, life actually sucks sometimes and there's nothing you can do about it.'* I choose to think otherwise.

Affirmation: *I scan my body for lessons to learn.*

Inner Child

I can find my inner child again, my little girl, and hear the truth through my body and acknowledge the pain.

I sit with her and tell her I'm here. I tell her there is wholeness and beauty in me without needing anyone else. I let her know she's *always* connected to everyone in the universe.

By experiencing moments in life that feel like they shatter you into millions of pieces, I remember, it's still all me—beautiful and whole, and even more exquisite to share with the world than before.

Affirmation: *I know my inner child is always with me, trusting me to be the guide.*

The Loop

"No, not only that!"

How many times have I felt on the continuous loop, the challenge of balancing everything just on the brink of collapse? For me, it took time to grow out sideways and down-ways and back up-ways again.

Negativity is like a storm, an indoor rainstorm.

Do I even have the right equipment to weather it? Where can I buy such gear?

It took me *many* storms to recognize I should actually go out and get some 'gear.' Sometimes the weather can bruise, other times, it can leave you feeling cold and alone. Either way, I've been thinking about how to get my gear. I have no idea, but I have some twinkle of hope that maybe I know already, that I just need to get more still. Dive in and breathe and let it come to me, maybe through my friends, my creativity, my past experiences. Those might be the start to the gear.

So yes, maybe I do know where to get it. We can prepare ourselves for *some* of life's storms. Not all of them.

Then it's just figuring out how to put on the gear.

Affirmation: *Today, I stay still to learn what tools I have to weather the storm*

Who Cares, Anyway?

At this time of day, late-afternoon, I try to just sit and be still. I don't really go quiet in my head at all, but my body just doesn't want to budge. Especially when my dog is curled up next to me; it's snuggly and warm and quiet. I think, *count your blessings.*

I want to be able to bottle up this peace. Somehow the minute the parenting job is back on the clock, there is no peace for me to drink up from any bottle. Most moms probably just think about the wine bottle. ☺

The first snow arrived this weekend and it was really nice actually. We were outside quite a bit and got lots of fresh air, with the kids caroling, which included lots of yelling and arguing, but I'm going to mark it down as a success. The people whose doors we knocked, were so pleasantly surprised—We haven't had carolers in over twenty-five years!

My youngest had a great line last night I don't want to forget. We were at hibachi and the chef was starting to cook and I said, "Smells good." My oldest said, "I can't smell anything yet," and his brother said, "The only thing I smell is pure entertainment!" It was priceless. He has a gift for putting a smile on people's faces; he's filled with peace and joy when he isn't concerned about anything. Another tidbit, lately, is at night he tries to slow down my singing at bed and he says, "See, I knew I could slow you down." Isn't that true, my love? A pure gift for sure.

My oldest and I are back to battling a bit too much again. It's just all the little things that add up to being really difficult to be around—singing, humming, talking, asking questions, touching everything… sort of back to that sensory overload type kid. And I tried to take them sledding and climbing to help with his body to do some heavy work, but not sure it helped calm his central nervous system at all. He did seem tired this morning, but a bit on edge.

My youngest has been so patient lately with the battles. He's even trying to teach his brother—*think about the people around you.* Another growth for him.

So then my miracle boy shares his light, I smile and take a moment to thank God. Maybe that's my gratitude for today, his light. And it's okay it's just one of my kids, right?

Why does it feel odd that I need some kind of positive affirmation from both, to feel progress, when I'm being given all this light?

Affirmation: *I am thankful for the miracles that can happen in the smallest of moments.*

Needs and Wants

Part of the fuel that drives the giver in me is the full sense of good I feel when someone needs me and I can help. Someone, say my son, or my hubby, needs help, I give them said help, and they are happy, thus I am happy.

Something about this gets broken down if the end result is not happiness.

Someone needs help, I try to help, it doesn't work—shit, I'm a failure! They aren't happy; I'm not happy.

The raw need of someone else relying on me is invigorating, as long as I can give to them what they need. But two things could be happening in this scenario that I'm trying to open my eyes to. One, my son isn't learning how to rely on himself. Two, (shocker) I'm not learning how to rely on myself. I'm feeding my emotions with someone else's, going hungry when I fail. The classic, teach a person to fish, instead of feeding them the fish.

I have a way to go with this learning. I go blind to this one way too easily, the giver in me taking over. I'm trying to start with the simple things:

Son: "Mom, can I have a glass of water?"
Me: "Yes, you may, you know where the glasses are."

And even while saying that, the power of my giver is tugging so strongly, whispering twisted thoughts in my ear:

Maybe you should get the water for him. He seems like he needs love. If you don't give him the water, you aren't being a good provider for him.

He needs to know he's being taken care of by you, you should get him the water.

Sneaky girl, that giver Liz, it's almost enough to convince me.

But I've grown. She can hang around and toss these thoughts into the vapor and I will distill them to useful ones.

My true knowing speaks: *My son might need some love and attention, and after he gets his water, I'll ask if he wants to play a game with me.*

But even before that, I check in with my little Liz and ask, "How are you doing? Do you have enough energy to give some love to the boy?"

And I wait and listen, honoring my truth as it is.

Affirmation: *Today, I check in with myself before giving of myself.*

Self-Care

I just put the boys to bed. I'm about even keel, still a little charged when I'm not being heard or things aren't going the way I expect. I need to sit with that a bit, but I recognize that a day like the one I had—yoga in the morning; ease into shower; a couple easy errands; haircut; a calm walk, before the boys got home made the rest of the day balanced. By bedtime, I don't have too much stress. It feels like if I didn't have all of that support and self-care, I may not have made it to the end of the night.

What do I make of that?

I'm starting to remember why it didn't feel so completely impossible after my divorce. It's because every minute I had alone I was doing something FOR ME—filling myself up.

I can't lose sight of that.

Affirmation: *Today, I keep a close eye on self-care, honoring all that I may need.*

Love Matters

I took my sons to a Black Lives Matter march today. My oldest son, fully swimming in the deep end of puberty, and afflicted with the binary (no gray) brain of autism, asked me about George Floyd—*So, is it because he was black that the police treated him the way he did? How do people know that's why he was treated that way? Why would the color of his skin matter?*

My gut reaction was visceral, my mind raced—*it matters!* We cannot let injustice continue. We cannot allow inequality and the treatment of humans to be different based on race. Then I take a breather. Maybe he really doesn't see how this could ever happen? Maybe before this, he thought we were all treated equally?

Then my ego plays the fun game of 'guess how Mom failed?' I criticize myself silently with thoughts like: *where did I go wrong? You haven't done anything to educate them. How could he ask such a simple question when it's so obvious? Are my children under the veil of white supremacy so much that the veil is turning them blind?*

Maybe I'm being somewhat harsh on myself because conversely, I can wish upon the world the simplicity of the view of my autistic son, one where everyone really is treated equally. End of story, right?

The real curious part will be when my son is witness to injustice in action. What emotions will it provoke, fear, anger, confusion, astoundment? And how many of us have our eyes open enough to see it happening? If we don't submerge ourselves in diversity of all kinds, how can we practice true humanity. Exposure is necessary. Action is required. Love, compassion and openness will be the way to lift us from this heaviness.

Affirmation: *I live with love, compassion, and openness.*

Boundaries

We grow up learning the world's expectations upon us. What do our parents expect, what do our friends expect, what do our teachers expect, and the fitting-in becomes an exercise of comfort and belonging. I've learned that this exercise is actually shackled. And I've spent a good part of my life breaking free of those shackles. I've learned the warning signs, mostly from my body, to when I need to place boundaries and focus on self.

Life can still get in the way though, my old habits can sneak back in. Today, I found myself overwhelmed with too much to do and too little time, and seemingly no one to help.

As I went through my list of things to do to figure out the highest priority—what could I possibly skip; how to I maintain self-care—I realized that the boundaries I've put up to protect my self-care, I have yet to set for myself. It's not the external world's expectations that are putting pressure on me it's actually my own expectations.

Driving back from an errand, I realize the stigma I'm fighting against is my own beliefs. My tricky people pleaser achiever has stepped into the driver seat again without me even knowing. I find myself sitting copilot, rubbing my eyes to lift myself out of my fog and looking over to the driver and saying, *what the f---?*

Get out of my seat! I am the driver here, not you. Please feel free to take a seat in the back. I will not kick you to the curb but I will take the wheel.

And then a miracle happens with that realization, the overwhelming feeling washes completely away. I don't *have* to do anything. Honestly. What is it I'm capable of achieving today? One breath at a time trying to keep my eyes wide open, and staying behind the wheel.

Affirmation: *I acknowledge the healthiness of setting boundaries and look to honor those I create for myself and the external world.*

Loving Me

When I think about past loves, I see my younger-self clinging on to hope, though it's controlled by the fear of abandonment. Today, it's about loving myself, and trusting my inner thoughts telling me I'm okay, I can be alone, and I will always have love.

It feels good to love myself. Especially without the younger-self clinging to any one relationship. It's not to say I don't still struggle with the unfortunate absolutism of a black and white mind sometimes taking over with the 'all or nothing' choices.

Here's what I do know:

I know there is an in-between.

I know I can trust myself.

I know I will never be alone.

I know I will do whatever is needed to help my children grow into kind adults.

I know I am capable of extreme empathy and compassion.

I know I love me.

Affirmation: *I am loved.*

I Can Be All Things

I can be many things: I can be powerful; I can be an important corporate woman leader; I can be a single mom to very complex children: I can also be a hippie. Or lazy. Or motivated. Life isn't so much about choice. It's about our reaction, our thoughtful, soulful, pause-to-check-in-with-your-inner-knowing reaction.

My emotional stability is built on my childhood and I can't fault my experience for any lack of preparation. Rather, I can learn how to open to it, right now. In the next moment, I can be conscious enough to see the emotions coming and ride the waves.

In order for my voice to be heard, I have to be okay with the response—any response to any version of myself, I also have to be okay when it's time to shut up and listen to my inner child.

She will be the ultimate light to show the way.

Meditation gets me closer to my inner child and to stillness: in stillness comes the knowing and a lot of emotions to flow. But then, I've learned not to build a damn but to open the floodgates for that emotion to live. And… it's all okay.

Societal stigmas—the way I was programmed—will take a lifetime of relearning, but before then, I will spend as much time as I can with my inner child to get to know my truth, the one God gave in completeness when I was born.

Affirmation: *Today, I am all things, complete.*

Journal Exercises: Family

Our upbringing and family unit we came from, and where we are today, play such an important role in our self-care journey. Use the following themed journal exercises to conduct your own self-discovery and start your awakening:

1. In what ways have you forged a new path out of your own difficulties? What does it mean to you when you face moments that you lack control? How do you cope? Do you? (Ref: Anxiety; Turning Pages).

2. Even though each of our stories are unique, the ideas of 'enough' and 'shoulds' and 'success' can all be ones we can peel back and investigate. Write about the things in your life you need to peel back in order to 'just be.' (Ref: Achiever; Pleaser, Pumpkin Eater)

3. What in your upbringing might be holding you inside containers? Let your writing flow through your internal script. Reflect on what it says: do you notice any shame or criticism? What are some of your core values that might need inspection? (Ref: Warning: Process this Slow; Life's Choices Are a Rubik's Cube).

4. What song brings you back to a significant moment in your life? Why did the song stop? What would it take to bring it back? Do you want that song to play again? (Ref: The Day the Music Died).

5. What experience(s) have made you feel like you have lost time? Ever feel blind to reality or ever woke up feeling foolish? Take a deep breath and look within. Make a careful observation: who is it that's behind your driver's wheel? (Ref: Spiritual Divorce; Boundaries).

6. What do you wish for your children's lives? Do you tend to want them to strive for things/experiences that you didn't have? Why? Write about moments you regret in parenting or caregiving. Once on paper, what will it take to forgive yourself? What will it take for your turn treat these experiences as lessons? (Ref: Generation; Nothing to Fix).

THE EMOTIONAL WORLD

Emotions

Like a pebble in a stream, I am easily mobile.
My river of emotions can take me away.
Larger boulders need to hold me close to keep me steady.

I am older now, a stone in the river of my emotions.
Still riding the current with the need for support to stay still.

I am an adult; I'm a boulder in my river of emotions.

Watching the water flow, feeling each emotion but with a sense of
curiosity and observance. rather than letting it take me away.
I am steady in my river.
I am secure.

But imagine those pebbles that have no boulder to stop them?
Imagine those stones still getting taken away?
How do they learn to become steady?
How do they grow to be rooted?

Guide your little pebbles to accept their river flow.
Hold them close and let the water race over both of you.

Feel the power of your strength
in knowing how to let the river flow through you.

You are one with your emotions.
They cannot hurt you.
They will pass.
And you will remain.
Solid, secure, strong and true.

Guarded Emotions

Imagine you are a small pebble in a river—the river is symbolic for your emotions—and at any minute, it can be turbulent and unpredictable: you are small and you don't know how to deal with this river. Shouldn't there be a boulder to protect you, one that will hold you close and tell you, *it's okay.* The water is flowing hard now, but I've got you, this turbulence is natural; it will pass. But a child (or pebble) without that support just gets tossed around in the water, deciding perhaps the best thing is to find a way to dig deep in the sand.

All the inputs of emotions and sensitivity to keep the peace, is exhausting. I'm supposed to just *not* make things worse—that's my first goal. The second is to not make assumptions. We often assume things about one another, without seeing all sides. In the end, assumptions never get us anywhere. Thirdly, I've come to recognize I'm often on guard for emotions I don't even know exist.

It's like going about the day, while constantly feeling like a failure—even if the moment doesn't warrant it, that emotion is there, informing the situation. I want to help my kids, but in the end, they still have to face things on their own. No matter what I do, they can't avoid the conflicts and scenarios coming at them. Am I a failure if they fail?

What I take away is the love I bring them. Failure or not, it will always be me and my boys against the world.

Affirmation: *Today, I let all emotions flow.*

Thinking the Worst

Is it normal to immediately think the worst when something is happening that you cannot fully understand?

Some call it 'negativity bias,' but faced with an unfaithful husband, an inner dialogue starts:

o   Was there more than one woman?
o   Was she already living with him?
o   Was his life with me too much to bear?
o   Is he hurt somewhere?

Are we loved, even when people leave? That seems to be the question masquerading in the others.

It takes trusting that God has my back. The Universe has my back. My family has my back. My friends have my back. And most of all, *I* have my own back.

I AM loved.

Affirmation: *I have my own back. I AM loved.*

Autumn

Is it easy for the tree to let go of its leaves? Or are they like tears falling down and saying goodbye? As I watch autumn unfold, with the sunlight casting prisms of light against a falling leaf, I can't help but believe Mother Nature is saying, "I honor you. Thank you. Now, let it go." How can we shed what we need that easy? What in our world can act as the breeze to gently tug at all that doesn't serve us and help us release to the flow?

I consider moments available to us: a good conversation with a friend; getting connected again with a spouse; being still to reflect and honor. There is no scientific research to this idea, but during the autumn season, when the trees are letting go of their leaves, they are also reaching their roots deeper into the earth, preparing for cold. They are relying on their foundations to move through the next phase of growth.

Who or what is your foundation to rely on? Do you find it with a friend, a pet, in nature, in God, or inside yourself?

We just need to be still and feel your roots and be the journey.

Affirmation: *My foundation is strong.*

Riding the Roller Coaster

Lately, I feel like I've been on someone else's ride. I'm so sensitive to the emotions of others around me, especially the ones I love most. My son loses his mind because his pants don't touch his ankles; I breathe. But then my other son stomps about, upset I didn't wake him up at the right time and I lose my cool.

I find myself so reactive to other loved ones' emotions, I almost can't distinguish my own.

Then in one of my brief moments of reflection—this time while driving—I think to myself, okay, I've owned the fact that I don't like rollercoasters. I recognize it's not a logical fear, but a phobia I'd rather not deal with. I share this phobia with friends and family and I'm still accepted, they don't shame me for it. ***Why then, do I feel the need to ride the rollercoaster of someone else's emotion?*** Why can't I stay with them at the (figurative) amusement park and assure them I will be there when they get off the ride and are ready to jump on the next? I'm still providing the love; I'm still not giving up on them. Isn't that enough? Why should I strap in for the ride?

So how about this: until I can deal with my own emotions, I shouldn't attempt to assume others'. It only ends in hyperventilation for us both, with them wondering how I couldn't be there for them, when I just needed to assure them, "I see how upsetting this is for you, and I'm here, and will be always."

Next time someone I love is erupting with emotion, I will take a deep breath and envision the rollercoaster cart ascending its steepest loop-de-loop, and realize, I am not on that ride. This is not my emotion to carry.

I can just be there for them, steady and loving.

Affirmation: *I hold my loved one's emotions close, but do not consume them.*

The Broken Vase

My great-grandmother's vase meant so much to my mother, as it signified the memories of their love. My son who had no awareness of the importance and is a clumsy boy to begin with broke it. Now what? I can empathize with my mother's connection towards the vase on an emotional level, but not the material one:

o   The vase is broken. It cannot be fixed.
o   This action does not change the memories of my mother and her grandmother but still provokes a deep sadness within her.
o   This action does not change my son's view on the world.
o   This action makes my son feel guilty but without understanding why, and the emotion is as fleeting as the waves rolling ashore.
o   I watch the action and feel the emotions of all of my loved ones crashing about.

I watch. I am on shore.

The act of breaking the vase is done, but the emotions of individuals involved based on their prior experiences are locked in and branded in their memory banks for the next experience for this same emotion to rise.

How can I help my loved ones come to shore, to the freedom of it?

How we react to the experience is within our realm of control. Even if the emotional instinct is one of sadness, fear, anger. Those are all natural and welcoming, but we can let them flow and not hold them tight.

The energy it takes to hold on is tiresome and wasted while the rest of life continues on.

Affirmation: *I approach experiences with a space for observation before reaction.*

An Emotional Fable

Stubbornness is a funny thing.

It's very friendly with righteousness.

They are buddy-buddy.

Stubborn: "Hey, don't be the first to say anything or do anything that might show you care."

Righteous: "Exactly, because then it will seem like we're admitting we're wrong, and we both know we're right."

Stubborn: "Yes, we need redemption and will wait on this mountaintop stoically waiting for that to come."

Righteous: "Of course, they need to understand, we were right and they must learn."

So Stubborn and Righteous wait on top of the mountain with their chests puffed out and their noses in the air, waiting for the other to change. Before long, there is wind and rain, to knock them off balance. Their backs are getting tired from standing up so straight and their feet hurt with such a solid stomp in the ground.

How long will stubborn and righteous wait?

How long do you let yours?

Affirmation: *Today, I let these emotions rest; honoring them, but not allowing them to take over.*

Righteousness

Why do we get a positive feeling inside when we are right about something? Where does that need to be right come from? Does everyone feel like that when they are right or is it just people like me?

We get caught in sticky situations where we want to be right no matter how it makes someone we care about feel, at least for a fleeting minute. How open and vulnerable can we be to change and be accepting of other perspectives with this seemingly animal instinct?

Affirmation: *Today, I catch myself from letting righteousness take over.*

False Positive

Happy is not something I trust too easily nowadays. What I'm realizing is that trust actually goes way down if there is alcohol involved. I have this internal script that says, "Well, they are only acting this way because of the wine."

Be careful, this is touchy ground.

As I peel back my onion, I make sure my little self has room to breathe. I ask her, "What's going on here?" My answer reminds me I grew up with a family unit who thrives on fun.

We vacationed to great places.
We had a summer home.
We had Halloween parties and other parties.
We camped.
We had a lake house.
Growing up, I lived in this blur of joy.

I knew my parents drank alcohol, and I definitely followed suit once peer pressure kicked in during high school. It all felt very FUN. Good fun.

But those make it or break it moments of incremental trauma were never allowed. No other emotion or attitude was allowed into Fun Zone! But who wouldn't sign up for a lifetime membership to that—the glory of family fun, and friend fun, and grown-up fun, seemingly all the time?

I still naively crave the FUN, only it's more like Pinocchio being lured by the wolf to all the fun and games. The whole time Pinocchio could see he was turning into a donkey, his own self-reflection—*why isn't this right?*

Today, I wonder how I can be scared of fun so easily. It feels like walking on a Jell-O floor. It always returns to the same conclusion, the classic, 'When's the shoe going to drop?' phenomena. If there is fun by someone I love, mostly just family, my warning flags are raised that I'm about to be lost, unheard, not allowed to show any other emotion besides joy. It seems like instead of going along for the joyride, I dig my heels in and make sure I kill the buzz. My bitchiness and bitterness get cranked up and my walls go up—this fun is fake, do not allow in, *danger, danger!*

Being an observer of it is new and feels like a good step in the right direction.

Affirmation: *My past does not define my future. I live in the present and let love flow.*

Playing with Fire (Spoken from Anger's Perspective)

I'm here but I'm scared.

I've never been allowed to start my fire and I keep getting drowned in water.

I'm afraid my light and warmth can never be shone.

Without me, you've gone starving, because you need fire to eat food, to nourish your body and soul.

Without me you've been drowning. I want you to come to our campsite and sit around the fire.

You do not need to fear me, because I'm here to keep you warm. I'm here to feed you.

I'm here to ritualistically unleash the burdens you carry—just like the aboriginal people start bush fires to protect their trees.

I'm here to protect you. Come to the circle, come to the fire, sit and be. All will be okay.

For all of time, I've felt you don't trust me to give you the protection you need. I've felt you drown me in fear that my fire will get out of the control and take over—but only by avoiding me can that happen.

Avoiding is feeding it more oxygen to keep growing, instead of just letting me be to do my job.

When trusted, I provide you your passion, your drive, your determination, your persistence.

Sit with me at the fire. Trust *all* is the way it needs to be and release your fear.

Affirmation: *Today, I allow all emotions, including anger, to flow.*

Corona Bliss

I'm having this visceral reaction to people posting about how life is so easy. Not a care in the world, just hanging out remarking, "Look at us 6-feet apart—aren't we special? Aren't we rule followers with style?"

And it's happening all around me. I see kids literally huddled together shoulder-to-shoulder for hours and then a post about 'social distancing.' It's raising my heart-rate.

So I have to pause and ask myself, why I'm getting all worked up about it? A few words come to mind: jealousy, judgment, shame, fear, lack of belonging, isolation...

People seem to be coping with these very raw, very real emotions with humor, which I guess is our human nature, and gives a little light to the darkness. For me, it feels manufactured. The 'we are in this together!' or let's make a sign or write on our sidewalk, seems fake. Again, my ego might be taking over, I completely understand it, but I have no energy for sidewalk chalk. I have no joy for funny posts. I am literally living moment by moment and pretty damn proud of that. But it's nothing to post about. It's nothing to share with the world: we are in this together! I'm here, on my couch, breathing—oh, you're breathing too? Oh damn, I'm not alone then? But instead, I feel a victim to the competition of 'coping.' Who has it worse? Those who don't, get inside, please.

I don't know what matters. Does it really matter if my kids are outside with eight other kids in a huddle all day? They didn't go to the grocery store, does that count? They didn't get gas or help someone at the hospital. So why does it bother me so much? Is it the rule abider in me, the eternal, *do no wrong and make everyone else do right* belief-system chiseled into me? Maybe.

Affirmation: *I take the time to assess my current beliefs, without judgment, and recognize those which no longer serve.*

Change is Hard

I was brought up with the magic of Christmas morning at its best: a glowing tree with what seemed like hundreds of presents underneath, overflowing into the room, though in actuality, it was a modest array of essentials.

One year to surprise the boys, I gave each of them individual Play-Doh and Hot Wheels and then one large box for both of them.

As they tear open the box, they discover a notebook with the label on it, 'My first trip to Disney!' It takes them both a second to realize what it meant: a trip to Disney World.

My anticipation is immense—almost as much as theirs opening it and making the discovery. I had imagined their excitement a hundred times over—not to mention what we'd do on the actual trip, including them smiling as they journaled their fun time.

But that's not what happened. Instead, they complained!

They wanted to play with their new toys; they wanted to hang out with their friends during the holiday break; they didn't want the change—in fact, they got into pure resistance mode.

I share this story with teams because even when we think we have something *amazing* to go towards, something new and exciting, our human circuits are wired to resist, to stay in the current flow we are in. The shift is where the pain is, no matter how amazing and beautiful what you are shifting to can be. Not only that, but our best-laid plans, may not work for everyone.

Even a trip to Disney can cause someone to complain.

Affirmation: *It's natural to resist change. I allow space for this resistance to pass and do not take offense to it.*

The Ego

I'm curious about the concept of the ego and trying to move away from it towards the light of love. What about characteristics like ambition, drive, wanting to succeed—are these all ego-based? And does that mean that they are false or bad?

Logically, it seems right to say choose love instead of fear. Choose love over pain. Choose love over struggle. But when it comes to choosing love over achievement, or goals, or ambitions it starts to seem like complacency instead of love. Is that why surrender is so hard? It's not surrendering from fear to love but rather surrendering from the falseness the ego projects, even the seemingly good stuff?

Also, I can't get my head around letting my inner spirit guide me and how that might conflict with when I try to set goals, make plans or decisions. Does it mean those things are false projections as well and there is no purpose in goals, plans, and decisions?

I guess it comes down to control. I want to make a plan and have goals to feel in control of my path. The question then becomes can I truly relinquish that control to a higher source and trust the path that's already there. Honestly, that's when fear really kicks in for me. It might mean I'm on the right track in exposing my ego. If I don't spend time making a plan or setting goals, what am I doing with myself? If those are activities I actually truly enjoy, maybe I can do those activities as a job and have it be my own path.

Affirmation: *Today, I truly relinquish control to a higher source.*

Bravery Doesn't *Need* to Equal Tough

I've been reading a lot about women and how we are raised to be perfect, people pleasers and that the alternative is to be brave. I'm getting wrapped around the axis with the notion that bravery means being tough. There are examples for this hypothesis like a girl standing at the top of a high diving-board and being afraid, and her parents coddling her and not pushing her, while if the same thing happens for a boy they just say, "You can do it! Come on!"

The suggestion is that if as children, girls were raised the same as boys that perhaps they would be braver and more willing to fail and try again. Something just doesn't resonate with me with this hypothesis. It's the fact that emotional vulnerability is the factor we are not willing to allow.

What would happen if instead, all children were coddled equally?

Does bravery have to be a big thing you fear? Or can it be *admitting* your fear, asking for help and working through it?

It seems to me, the bravest moments I've witnessed from my children (boys) are when they let the tough (fake) armor down and had a good cry, admitting they are scared and didn't know what to do. Same goes for my tribe of women. I see the bravest souls admitting they are lost, not knowing how to get through it, but seeking to be connected with each other in the journey. That's bravery to me.

Admitting we're scared seems most brave of all.

Affirmation: *I will ask for help and be brave in doing so.*

Beauty

How do you define beauty?

Conventionally, we are taught that appearances are in the eye of the beholder. I've learned that allowing only one of my five senses to define beauty is incomplete. I grew up being told how beautiful I was, as a little girl, the adults around me applauded me for my beauty—*my how beautiful you are!* Then when I didn't get similar attention from my peers, I was convinced my beauty wasn't there. Like it was all a made-up ploy from the adults to make me feel good. As I grew a bit older, I did start getting attention from peers for my beauty, which reinforced that I was being defined by appearance.

This misconception of looks fed into young children, especially girls, has now caused me pause, because I see my children's generation continuing the stigma: the confirmation that beauty is external, and that it equals attention, hence love. Everyone wants love, and in turn, we reach for beauty by any means possible. We straighten our hair, pluck our eye brows, wear the trendy clothing.

I have since relinquished this torch. No longer do I need to 'look' for beauty as something my eyes will see. It doesn't negate the visible beauty there is all around, nor should it be the only definition.

Things I define as beautiful:
o   A friend holding my head in her lap as I cry over something seemingly insignificant.
o   A dad saying sorry to his children for messing up and admitting he's still learning and growing.
o   A connection with a person I've only met once (in-person), who has helped me find my true path in life.

Our beauty is all around us. Honor it. Share it No products required.

Affirmation: *My inner beauty shines through for all to receive.*

Living Wild

We could take a page from our fellow mammals on how to live. Maybe then, some of life would be much simpler. We could start by trying to meet our basic needs like food, shelter and sleep, and grant ourselves time to play. Do the work and leave it.

As I watch my dog all day, seeking attention for affection, connection, play, food and then rest, I realize life is this simple and complete. How do we get back to these basics? How can we awaken to this and return to ourselves the way God is intending? No shame, no judging, just be human.

Perhaps as children we start out wild, untamed. I see it with my children for sure, my attempts to tame them to society's picture frame, they will not oblige. Their resistance to being tamed ignites such an amazing fire within me. That fire is mostly fueled by shame, embarrassment, and fear that they will never be accepted.

Why am I requesting they be accepted by anything other than themselves? We don't need to be accepted; we just need to be *true*.

What if all we were *truly* destined for is to give love and affection to others? Is it our egos or our intelligence that gets in the way? Achievement, social expectations, progress, comparison, are all structures we created for the human race to live within. We could do more by living wild.

Affirmation: *Today, I go back to basics and enjoy the simple life.*

Hey, Jealousy

Jealousy has been casting its net over my world. I see others being busy and productive. I sit restlessly and think, "Should I be doing more?"

I see how others are creating things with their children, sending out signs of gratitude, filling their days with board games, outdoor fun and arts and crafts. Jealousy comes knocking—*why aren't you doing that? Why can't you have a family life like that?* Even the simplest moments where people are talking and laughing together, my friend, jealousy, just hops in laughing and snickers, "Yeah, must be nice."

What am I supposed to learn from it?

All that seeking, is not unattainable. I could go outside and rake, or get the art kits out and get my kids outside. I could call friends or walk next door and chat with neighbors to smile and laugh. But something holds me hostage. Something is holding me back—that's the most curious part. Because I've always believed that jealousy can be an emotion to fuel you to action, motivate you to seek what you desire. But I'm not motivated for that; I'm motivated to sit my butt down and read. To soak in the sun and be still.

To check in with myself, because I know from little experience of my awakened life, that it's me I need to be quiet and listening to. So is jealousy just old stigmas or old shame rearing up?

I'd like to think it's not so much jealousy, as it is different choices. Savory choices that have made me the person I am and love.

Affirmation: *I check in with myself and listen.*

How Are You Doing?

We are programmed to ask each other, "How are you doing?" We respond with a canned response, like *good* or *fine,* without any thought or true connection made.

I find when I'm talking to a close friend, one I haven't seen in a while, I shift my question to "How are YOU?" I'm attempting to connect deeper. To me it sounds a bit more connected. What strikes me is how we need to add the word 'doing,' as if we're always fixated on *doing* things and getting things done. We don't spend enough time in the present and just *being.*

When I visited Australia, I got used to saying, "How ya going?" Perhaps the culture is more focused on the journey? In Japan, it's customary to simply ask, "Daijobu?" It means, "Are you okay?"

My awakening has been caught up in the conversation of *being* vs. *doing* for quite some time. The hypothesis that my body kept trying to prove is that part of the self-care journey is pausing to just be. I do sincerely believe I've proven this hypothesis time and again when I run myself to the ground holding everyone else up and not giving myself the time I need. But during the conversation, one thought weighs in: "But DOING exercise or DOING a craft or DOING something you love is good right?"

Why would we stop DOING just to BE?

Today, this circling plane of conversation in my head has finally landed. It landed in a field of creativity. Where the act of DOING is ALWAYS inspired and joyful. And yes, this can mean exercise, or baking, or writing or any other ING besides Be-ING.

Because in this field of creativity, it's our BEING that is engaging in the activity. Our being that is motivated to create or move or connect. The motivation doesn't come from the *should;* it doesn't come from others; it doesn't come from any societal construct—it's within us!

That's where the true act of Being walks down the aisle to join hands with Doing.

This field is sacred and full of joy and hope, love and rest. It conjures a tingling of wholeness when these two are connected.

No longer is it a debate of either-or, *doing* vs. *being*, but rather, the matrimonial infusion that happens when you've found your calling.

Then we can lay in the grass looking up at the clouds, smiling in gratitude that today, your plane has landed in this field.

Affirmation: *I find my creative spark and rejoice in its beauty.*

Black and Blue

When our body gets hurt and bruised it gets swollen and red. Then over time, it actually gets darker: a purplish, black color takes over.

I imagine emotional-hurt the same way. The emotional pain can make us feel swollen, a sort of fullness with rage. Then over time, it actually feels like a darkness has been cast. Depression can set in. What we might not realize is the necessity of this darkness.

Just like a bruise on our body, darkness is a natural part of the process to healing. When embraced, simply take some deep breaths, and trust in the flow of the universe.

Affirmation: *My body holds all, I listen to what it has to teach.*

The Cards You Were Dealt

You can only do as much as what you've been given.

Is that true? People get dealt a bum set of cards and they're out of luck and can't change it. Is it true, if we get a winning hand, to not let on that you have something good—it could be taken away, or you might feel bad for the others knowing there's no chance against your hand?

We let life happen this way sometimes. Sometimes, we have everything, at least everything we need at that moment. But we are busy trying to shame ourselves by saying we don't deserve it, or we frighten ourselves that it's only going to happen this *one time* or hide it deep down, and can't truly embrace the joy.

Now, imagine you're dealt a *really* crappy hand. You know it. You also have to stay cool and not let on because maybe you can pull off a bluff. So you play the game. You see how far you can go with this bluff. And the further you get bluffing, the more manufactured joy is triggered in your body—*omg*, maybe I can actually still win with nothing!

And maybe you do.

That round.

Or maybe you are such a superb bluffer, you win round after round. Do you start to think there is a chance you can't lose?

A woman I know got her degree. She got the job and is raising her children, all while bluffing her success. Because what she doesn't realize is the success is in owning your truth, and owning the process of the game, not the winning or losing. She's made a lifetime out of how to manipulate and negotiate and control her bluffs, that when she loses, the absolute rage and despair is immense. Now we always knew what hand was dealt to her, from her parents, her upbringing, her childhood experiences, but because of the illusion of success, the truth of who she was kept so hidden, so afraid, so raw and vulnerable; when it gets exposed, it's like exposing a newborn to a blizzard without clothes on.

And what about the rest of the people playing the game? They've either learned their truth and are just playing for fun, or they are also swept up in whatever emotion is driven by the cards they were dealt. Depending on which, will determine how they handle their success.

It's up to all of us to accept our hand we've been dealt. Honor the truth of what it provides and enjoy the game!

Affirmation: *I stay lighthearted and enjoy the game of life.*

Anticipation

It's a funny feeling, anticipation. Not an easy one to sit with. We get busy and ready for whatever it is we are anticipating to come. Cleaning the house, cleaning ourselves, going through the list of what needs to be done ahead of time. I believe it might all be ways for us to avoid the feeling. The jitters… the butterflies... the fear... not knowing how it will go, *whatever* 'it' is.

On this particular day, I'm currently waiting for my stepdad's memorial to start. It's in three hours, and I'm running through my list, trying to stay busy. I can't help but feel bad that this isn't the way someone's passing should be (there's that *should* word again). We can't all be together because of COVID-19. We won't share stories in any organic way, while mingling with appetizers and drinks. We won't secretly wish we were alone to remember and grieve. We are already alone. And we waited a few weeks since his passing to have this memorial to what? Get everything lined up? All the ducks in a row? The organized, planned manner to which we address death feels manufactured to me. The moments before death, the time to say goodbye, that was organic.

We came together, if only a small few, and we leaned on each other. Then the stigma of what *should* happen kicked in. If rewriting my own will, I might just order people to all go out to a nature trail for the day, to sit or stand, and reflect on my life and my impact on them. I could write in a few questions: I'd want them to ask themselves how they can live and JUST BE.

The power of that silence and that collective energy of positive, loving thoughts, would connect me to them through the spiritual divide.

And sort of be fun to force people to stay still. ☺

Affirmation: *I can sit with the uncomfortable and honor the raw power.*

Restless

Summer solstice was yesterday. This time of year draws me towards outdoor music, sunshine, and joy. But with everything I'm trying to do, the day of rest comes with a deep restlessness. It's in my stomach. It's unsettling. Nothing in my mind can figure it out. My mind is flipping through the Rolodex of ideas:

Should I clean?

Should I be outside in the sun?

Should I do more at the shop?

Should I read?

Many questions, no answers.

Restlessness brings paralysis. It's an odd cocktail—feeling stuck, immobile—while also holding a sense of uncomfortable motion inside my bones. Maybe movement might help my brain says to myself, but my body stays still.

Do you ever feel like you are just wasting time? That there is something that would be better than stillness? But the pendulum swings fast, because the minute my time is demanded upon me by work, kids, my business, I regret not having more *downtime.*

Affirmation: *I let my body guide me, so the noise of thoughts isn't as loud.*

Whining or *Wine-ing*

Do you get weepy when REAL life happens?

What is it about those moments when someone truly supports you, either through an open ear, a helping hand, a trusted opinion, or just when you observe the simple moments that seem to burst open the heart, that make me weepy? Almost as soon as my tears form, I'm shaking myself for being so emotional, for letting someone see my weakness. It's what I've been taught. Emotions are weak and no good for decision-making or trust-building or confidence-building. Why was I taught that? Was there another way?

I'm wrestling with the idea of drinking alcohol a lot these days. I've found more likely than not, I desire a glass when I'm in a good mood. I'm analyzing this desire from all angles. For some reason, it feels like it's *not* all right, like it's a sin of some sort, but I can't figure out where that notion comes from. I don't have childhood memories of alcoholism and it turning life upside down. I also notice that my body craves it and wants to continue to imbibe well past when it's healthy. When I have the house to myself, I get to treat myself with a book, a chic-flick, a bath, anything I want, including a glass of wine—I got to dance and cook today, and I can relish in the quiet, clean home that I have—why is that bad?

Am I avoiding something else, like I've seen others do? I remember through many stages of grief and depression; alcohol was the last thing I turned to. Should I be doing more internal inventory to make sure I'm not missing anything?

Maybe this is one of my all-time favorite playlists, the 'all or nothing' mentality. I'm wrestling because I'm forcing my brain (and body) to decide—should I have alcohol, *yes or no...* is there no room for moderation over elimination?

There's a hole in the theory. The reason for joy isn't from the wine, it's BECAUSE I TOOK CARE OF MYSELF. So, you know what, folks? —*CHEERS!!*

Affirmation: *I do not let past stigmas drive present decisions.*

Flag at Half-Mast

The symbolism of a flag at half-mast always hits home for me. The representation of loss, mourning, and unity in that reflection, I've always found powerful.

I always pause when I see a flag at half-mast. As someone who doesn't stay in touch with much outside my family bubble of six, I don't always know what's going on in the world all the time and that's okay—who says we need or *should*. In fact, I'd argue we need less of it, in favor of more crucial time to be fully present with the people around us. Isn't that what the pandemic has shown us?

There's an unspoken rule as to what deems the lowering of the flag—a loss of a president, another mass attack on civilians—but I wonder, does the state of despair our country is in, during mass deaths from the pandemic, justify the flag be lowered?

Perhaps this symbol will speak louder than many words to bring us together in peace with less hate.

Affirmation: *Joining in a collective mourning will heighten my connections.*

Dream Last Night

In my dream, I was taken back to my childhood home, trying to do my scavenger hunt (which also happens to be what I'm doing for my son today). I arrive and my cat/dog chased a squirrel and killed it. I find a wrapped-up garbage bag chopped up half body, then just a head, so very gruesome.

Emotions were mostly just frustration, trying to get my thing done and having all these obstacles get in the way.

There was no fear, just annoyance.

I lifted the bagged body and thought—*really, could I just get this scavenger hunt done without another obstacle?*

What's interesting is that the dream didn't feel complete, so I kept wanting to go back to sleep and finish. There was no fear, the death wasn't scary, which was even more confusing for me.

There were also multiple ways to get around my house. The two flights of stairs to the deck. This isn't the reality of my backyard, but I've had dreams before where I've added onto the backyard like this, another section, and makes me think of the metaphors based on life experiences.

Perhaps the pictures of my childhood home are a window into my subconscious showing me just how well I handle stress and the unexpected.

Affirmation: *I let the window of dreams open my soul to healing.*

New Worlds Open

Creativity is like a spark. We need to catch it and take hold quickly before it goes out. For some reason there is this feeling of speed that coexists with creativity—must do this now! Must grab hold and not let go, until the spark goes out.

I've always said my son, who was diagnosed with Asperger's syndrome at age three—which I recently learned isn't a *proper* or *recognized* diagnosis anymore—was an evolved human. I believe, in the deepest part of me—my DNA you could say—that my genetics and his father's genetics, passed down through the generations, has evolved to a human on the autism spectrum. The beautiful formula of a little OCD-grampie, and ADHD-great-grampie, and abundant intelligence, has led to our amazing autistic boy.

Kids like him have a tough time in the 'gray,' the in-between, but what I've learned is that we ALL would prefer a bit of black and white. The *tell it like it is*, straightforward existence, that my son demands.

As a teenager, he's learned amazing coping skills for the 'in-between,' perhaps more than many of us can learn in a lifetime. That's because his mind is evolved. His spirit is evolved. Although he seeks the black and white—the setting of expectations met, the direct outcomes, his creativity lives in the beyond. He has calculated actions, calculated experiments, but they are driven by an unspoken creativity that I truly believe is mutated from us; he's one more tic on the evolutionary scale.

But this stretch in mind's capacity has put a strain on the spirit. Because his world hasn't caught up with his surreal framework, he gets lost in our colorful world sometimes. But the beautiful gift that we can learn, that I learn every day, is through his perspective, new worlds will open.

Although rigid in thought (sometimes), that rigidity can live amongst the most magnificent labyrinth of thought that you and I cannot fathom. So, although it's black and white, it does, in fact, already contain all the colors—and isn't that just the most amazing true glory of his spark?

In the end, if I try to limit his version of the world, of his 'black and white,' I'm actually limiting his creative spark. What I'd rather do is bask in his spectrum in awe of the new worlds opening in front of us because of his light.

I simply need to have faith in the unknown and let him lead the way.

Affirmation: *Today, I put no limits to my own creative spark.*

Pictures of Me

A picture can speak a thousand words—that's the phrase, right? Well, I'm no artist, so I'm sticking to words.

I'm trying to get used to sharing my thoughts with others, with the hopes that perhaps my thoughts are the same as any, who stay silent with the noise in their heads. As I venture into this world of social media, I'm realizing how much I might need to be comfortable with selfies. This is not my gig, my usual *picture.*

I currently have a pimple that has taken over my chin (who knew early menopause would cause acne) and who wants to see that? So I ask myself, what other way will people connect with me if they don't see my face? Is the selfie the new elevator pitch of who I am? And as much as I coach on people being able to explain in a couple seconds what makes them unique, the selfie feels WAY more vulnerable.

If I spend time looking pretty, before the selfie, it's not the authentic me.

Is my view of the selfie resistance to the new mainstream, or just resistance to exposing my true self?

Affirmation: *I stand brave in my vulnerability.*

Am I Seen?

On any given day I could be judged like a book cover in many ways:

Workdays: polished, professional, perhaps scattered, tired, energized, motivational, or inspirational.

Home days: definitely stressed, run-down, comfortable, at ease, confident, controlling.

Concert days: legs not shaved, clothes thrown on from whatever was available in the clean pile, alive, vibrant, carefree.

And based on these looks, conclusions would be made. I get to know folks at work and let them in on my dirty little secret of my carefree side and you can see their minds hitting a little bug in their system *does not compute.*

On any given day in public, folks could see carefree me (no makeup of course), and talk to me and find out, I am educated and own my own business and I see their brain trying to work things out—*does not compute...*

My look doesn't always match who others believe I am, but I'm here to tell you, *I am me*, no matter what I look like on the outside.

Shouldn't we celebrate all parts equally, instead of hiding some pieces of ourselves in corners and closets, for only those we trust?

I want to break down the paradigms of what a successful woman *should* look like. I can be polished, professional, well-spoken, compassionate, thoughtful, inspirational, and messy, tired, honest, direct, and stressed and it's *all me*—not one but ALL.

United I stand with ALL OF ME—hopefully makeup-free!

Affirmation: *I celebrate all the beautiful parts of me.*

Applaud Yourself

My dear friend just wrote—How are you so industrious? And give yourself no credit for doing so much?

I love how much we can learn from each other in the simplest of comments, the quickest of moments. Aren't we all industrious each day in some way? It might be the sheer effort of getting out of bed when depression has taken hold that we can call industrious, or it's the energizing tornado of checking off the to-do list. The most ironic is when we can admit we are being industrious with the difficult task of being still.

The achievers, like me, need things to be finished, before any credit is due. You don't get your grades until you hand in the paper. But what my friend has shone a light on is that this journey, this everyday industrious woman that I am and learned to love, is allowed credit for the journey.

It's on the path that the real teaching happens, not at the destination. Loving myself wholeheartedly means telling myself, "You're rockin' it, girl!" whether the list is being checked or not.

Affirmation: *Today I applaud myself on my path, whatever moment in the journey that means.*

Authentic Self

What I don't want:

o Mindless meetings that have no meaning and still take time and energy for no purpose.

o Crammed schedule where I'm just going from one thing to the next without even getting time to eat, bathroom, walk, breathe...

o Rushing from work to home without a break in between to reground for the next section of the day.

o Being caught in the 'glory' of being involved in what seemingly is 'more important': work. And losing sight of my priorities.

o I know my priorities are for me to find what fuels me—what gives me the energy to sustain the mundane and sometimes very difficult home-life that I want to be present for.

o Once I have an approach, how do I test that I'm prepared and can handle the real life I have to go back to?

o To focus solely on deadlines—because subconsciously it's driving me into the ground—*dead.*

What is non-negotiable:

o Being heard: supporting ways for people to truly be heard without being cut off.

o Diversity and inclusion.

o Mindful projects. To act.

o Knowing transitions are hard. Solicit the kids to help solve the problem.

o I want to spend time and teach the kids.

o Self-care. Self-advocacy: I need to feel in the relationship, in parenting, at work, as a daughter, as a friend, sister.

o   As an empath, ensuring I balance and recognize my emotions compared to others', and being open the self-care path needed to sustain me.

o   Self-discovery.

o   Time to read, research, write. Then test, learn and adjust.

o   Try something new each day. Could be the smallest thing.

o   Water is my element source of energy, use it!

o   Time to be in nature.

o   Time to laugh together.

o   Time to be in silence.

o   Time to help others.

o   Time to be analytical around human problems.

o   Time to be creative.

o   Time to watch children grow in their passions (e.g., sports, art, computers, outdoors, friendships, cooking.)

Journaling Exercises: The Emotional World

Getting to know the spectrum of emotions, allowing them in, and letting them flow, has been a long winding path on my journey. I've learned observation is a good place to start, openness is the key, and forgiveness is necessary. Let the following journal exercises help you tap into your flow of emotions.

1. How often do you feed off others' emotions? Do you get trapped on a ride? Write about a time you can reflect this happening. (Ref: Riding the Roller Coaster; The Ego).
2. Do you ever find yourself acting a certain way based on those around you without checking in if it aligns with your authentic self? Write about how you'd like to shift from autopilot to living fully awake. (Ref: False Positive; Corona Bliss).
3. Is there something in your life you feel is holding you hostage? Is there a societal stigma you are living within? How might you consider breaking free? (Ref: Hey, Jealousy; Change is Hard).
4. Write about a time in your life when you felt you didn't deserve something? What would happen if you allowed it to flow without shame or judgment? (Ref: The Cards You Were Dealt; An Emotional Fable).
5. What emotions are most difficult for you to accept? Why? (Ref: Playing with Fire; Thinking the Worst).
6. Write out your list of 'what I don't want' and 'what is non-negotiable.' Embrace all the emotions that will come to strive for your authentic self. (Ref: Authentic Self; Am I Seen?).

Moment with a Bird

I sit outside and let the sounds of nature wash away the world. I live in a place where noise has become constant. The cars on my street driving too fast, the echoes of the cars from the highway carrying their way to my backyard. Construction, yard work, planes—all a constant when I'm outside. But there is also chirping from so many different birds.

One of my favorite birds is the cardinal. I love how bright it is against the newly green bushes. He came to visit me today, while I was writing about jealousy and shame. He sat by me on a branch and started to sing his song. I noticed first by vision because he is so bright and vibrant, his song still a bit muffled against all the rest. But then I focused on his song and I sang back: a simple whistle to start the chain. Him, then me, then him again. And by the end of our duet, he let out a beautifully long-winded *goodbye*, with a puffed-up chest of pride.

I was honored to listen. In our conversation, I found my voice.

I found what I was searching for through all my jealousy and shame emotions—*just me*—wanting to be heard. That's it. So simple, yet the yearning for that is as large as the ocean. I call out too. And I realize, with beauty, it's easy to be *seen*. And I was raised to believe being SEEN is what to strive for, and being *heard* is not. Because being heard might mean I'm talking back, or not listening, or not doing as I'm told, being heard goes against the frame that beautiful woman is put inside.

I'm realizing maybe all my desire to teach and to write are all outlets to be heard. And in this *awakening*, my newly brave Liz is rebelling against criticism and judgment. I'll get there.

Right now, she's just trying to be heard; although, it's been so long her voice can either be really weak like the start of that cardinal's song or really loud and joyous, like the bird shared by the end of our duet.

I'll figure it out. I'm going to keep trying, keep exercising my voice, slowly and repetitively, until I can share for someone to listen and be honored in my song.

Affirmation: *I listen to nature for inspiration.*

Being Heard

I want to be heard.

I have an inner child who is having a tantrum because she has been neglected. She learned the only way to get attention was to be calm, cooperate. Be the perfect little girl. But what about the times when life was hard? What about the times when she needed to scream, or whine, or cry, or complain? She was not heard. She was not listened to.

It reminds me of a child's cartoon where a monster is going through the neighborhood causing havoc and it just keeps getting bigger and bigger, destroying everything around it. My inner child is that big monster. But she doesn't want people to run away screaming. She doesn't want people throwing things at her telling her to stop. She doesn't want to fight. She just wants attention, validation that what she is feeling is normal and even with the destruction, she is still loved.

So in my 'real' world, this comes out when I ask my kids to brush their teeth, over ten times, or turn off their devices, or any request I make of them, they don't comply, and my inner beast is activated, "I'm not being heard!" or "You must listen to me!" Without warning, without self-control, I lash out on the boys. I yell. I push. Then I cry. I say, I'm sorry, "Mommy is still learning too."

And then it happens with my hubby, through the wall he creates, one where I'm not let in. He shuts his door and my inner beast is activated. "I'm not being heard!" I retreat. I build my armor, preparing for the war that the emotions of abandonment make me feel.

I'm trying, inner child.

I see you now. I acknowledge you. I love you. I'm trying. And I will never give up. We will grow and be united in the wholeness of unconditional love, inside. A light that no one can dim. No one can touch.

I see our light growing. We are connecting. I won't leave you again. You will be heard.

Affirmation: *I honor all that my inner child has to teach.*

When We Need to Scream

My inner voice is screaming to be heard. I've used writing to express how it feels not to be heard and how it plays out in my everyday life with my kids and others.

Then I had a moment in the car with the kids this morning. They were telling me a story about their weekend at their dad's place. They invented a game where they go under each other's floats in the pool and try to flip them over. I become one of those cartoon characters where the monster rips out of my fake face, and I start yelling at them about how unsafe it is and how there was a boy who just got killed getting stuck under a float.

Now reflecting on my outburst later in the day, I know a few things:

1. I was scared and feeling out of control, which can quickly lead to anger and rage.

2. I blame my ex-husband for this lack of supervision which triggers shame and sorrow.

3. Since all of these emotions are ones that I wasn't taught as a child how to nurture, the feeling of neglect and incompetence rises which again makes me want to scream 'pay attention to me!' which is said from the little girl inside.

4. Because I'm consumed by the needs of my inner child, I'm not granting my own children the gift of good listening and discussion so they can learn about the potential dangers calmly.

All these observations collide and I realize something: perhaps when I've been writing about how desperately I seek to be heard, I could have

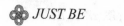

paused and actually LISTENED. I have the power to LISTEN to my own inner child.

Communication and caring and compassion don't always have to come from lessons and words, they come from just listening, and honoring the space to be.

That's my message to myself today.

Affirmation: *I am Okay.*

Persevere

I sit immobile. I know this is the word I need to write: persevere. As the letters mark the page those which stand out are SEVERE. So harsh. An aspect of cutting, severing ties, coping through struggle, all come to mind.

I thought that once I found my calling, my purpose, life would feel effortless. I've read of so many who found their calling and seem to find the flow to be freeing and empowering. I thought that living in my light meant I could avoid the shadows. Still, I'm driven by my inner child's fear of the dark. This lesson of surrender just feels so hard. Why does it have to be one struggle after another? Have I truly ever had to learn what it means to persevere? The ones who succeed through struggle, that we cast a medal of perseverance, is it only in their success that they are granted that accolade? Is the motivation of success, the idea of making it to the other side, what's supposed to keep me going? Lots of questions. Answers are still waiting to be received.

I thought that once I learned how to surf, I could ride all the waves. But life's crashing waves are thrashing me about every which way. It's a true test of letting go. With a limp body, the water will bring you to shore. The resistance to the crash, rigid and immobile, causes more pain. The waves crash about, the undertow is strong. The current of 2020 has taken many of us far away from the securities of our shore. I hesitate to write, 'why me?'

But seriously, WHY ME?

The victim role is not a character I like to play. In acting, it's fun to play the villain, even the jester, and most definitely the hero but the victim is my toughest character to accept. She wants pity, condolences, and someone to take care of her. She is weak. How could someone so weak

JUST BE

be trusted to perservere? That weakness is daunting for me. I'm afraid of it, if I show weakness, more loss might present itself.

I must acknowledge her, just like all the other cast of characters that make up me. The act of that recognition is the shift that's necessary. From rigid to flowing. Maybe what I need to do is severely TRUST. With that will come my true perseverance.

Affirmation: *I let the waves of life come and stay flexible to the flow.*

A Happy Grown-Up

I'm walking through my adult life feeling/thinking the same as I remember feeling when I was an adolescent. Does it mean that I grew up very fast, or am I missing something now? I walk around feeling like a fraud. Like I shouldn't be here—that I should still be taken care of like a child. I'm having a problem being a happy grown-up, constantly wanting to prove to people that I'm 'experienced' and 'know' things. That I want to be heard, listened to, provide guidance and help/support for others.

Maybe it's not the lack of my voice or being heard, and more the rub of being beaten down by those who are supposed to love me.

I remember the day, recently, that I went to my grandparents' gravesite. My Grammie embodied a woman with fierce strength in knowing herself. She was certain, smart, particular, calm, predictable, and kind. It wasn't until near the end of her life that I learned about her as a woman and not just as a grandmother. I remember when I turned twenty-one, she had a smirk on her face, and said very quietly, "Oh boy, when I was your age...".

She left her first husband, an alcoholic, with a new baby and very young. She worked driving materials to railroad workers through the woods before driving age in the 1920s. Her home had order and routine, which I gravitated towards, an always quiet calmness. My brother and I would be left there for overnights where we were treated with simple kindness and love.

I keep using the word 'simple' because that's as easy as I can explain: no fuss, no need to worry that I wasn't fitting in, or that I should make sure I act some particular way. I was allowed to Just Be. Maybe that's why I connect with her spirit so often now. Many other family members seemed to cast expectations and fuss about me. It could be positive— *my, how beautiful you are; look at those eyes!* which I took as the need to smile and be thankful of the compliment. Or it could be, *make sure you eat whatever they offer you. It would be rude otherwise,* I was told, which I took as the need to shove my own needs/wants aside for others.

But with Grammie, she let me be; she just stayed by my side. If a woman born in 1913 knew how to live her authentic-self at a tumultuous time in our country's history, I have hope for my own ability to do the same, with modern conveniences.

And the key to belonging, that she taught to me, is that sweet spot when we can love ourselves completely and be around others who let us be.

Affirmation: *I am learning how to live my most authentic-self.*

The Little Girl

I'm sorry, my little girl, says, bawling from inside. I cannot live up to your expectations. I cannot be the achievement focused girl you want me to be. I feel complete shame in not living up to these standards. I want to choose my path of light, but feel the shackles of guilt holding me back. The guilt that drives me to show up to my eight-to-five corporate-America job, the guilt that says I need to work hard, get paid well, support my kids' financial future.

I'm tired of letting the guilt drive the show.

My little girl is trying to let go. She's letting go of the guilt, but she is in fear and shame of doing so. I tell her it's okay to feel the way she does. It's okay to want to move into the light. I tell her I'm not going anywhere. I know this is so hard. The shackles are so tight around you.

Breathe. Let space in.

I see my little girl dressed in white, in an open field, dancing, boundless, but there is fear there too.

She asks: *"Why did you leave me? Let me come with you. Even though I bring my sadness, fear, and insecurities, let me be part of you."*

I reach out my hand.

I say to my little girl: *Have I told you lately I love you? Have I told you how inspiring, creative, joyful, innocent and lovable you are?*

Now I know, I can't let her be forgotten, she is my power, she is my warrior. Her fear will set me free once I stop running from her and hold her hand.

Together we will grow space from the shackles and one day they will just fall away. Until then, I'm here. I'm not going anywhere. No matter what you feel or do, you are loved.

Affirmation: *Breathe.*

Coming of Age

A well-known phrase for a transition in life that each of us goes through right around adolescence is *coming of age*. It's a time when our bodies, emotions, and thoughts are growing at lightning speed. When I read about other examples from characters in books living through this time, it seems to be presented as a type of looking back, like—*Oh, I'm here; I'm an adult; I see things differently, when did this happen?"* It's hard to pause, to see it transforming.

My children are on the brink of coming of age, so I haven't had the chance to observe someone else move through this part of life yet, but because it's fast approaching for them, I think I've been catapulted back to my adolescent years to journey through lost memories and investigate. I've begun to wonder: do we become an adult step-by-step over time, through small moments that add up, or is it thrust upon us during inconspicuous moments, only we can decipher later?

My childhood, as memory serves, was filled with joy, love and limitless possibilities for my future. I didn't spend much of my days in worry, anger, frustration, or torment. I did experience a great deal of loneliness. And now that I'm a mother, I think there is a knowing that even if a child isn't SAYING what they need or want, it doesn't mean they don't need or want it. I've been blessed with the gift of my children having *big mouths*, and are loud and clear about their needs. But I'm guessing, through my innate intuition, that I learned very quickly, when I was young, how to behave to be loved: follow the rules, be silent, self-sufficient, need-less, self-less, and love will remain.

Does that mean I was 'adulting' even then? Because it seems to me that this coming of age thing is really just a recognition of how one *should* be as they relate to the rest of the world. You become an adult once you behave with responsible actions as they relate to the rest of the world. You become an adult once you let silent thoughtfulness be your instinct before making decisions. You become an adult when you see your place as it relates to the rest of the world.

I was forced to be an adult the minute I assumed responsibility to be independent and selfless.

Much of the demand as an adult is based on how we fit within the world around us. *Why?* Can we be so naive to say that when we are 'grown up,' we will know how to handle ourselves around others? Isn't that just at the cost of losing our little self? Is our *true* self the light that shines at our birth or the learned adult we become? Perhaps when we are born, we are complete. Perhaps we don't require a 'coming of age,' but rather a 'becoming of self.'

I'd like to strive for this: to be a parent who my kids need for as long as it takes for them to find themself. Not to focus too much on their growth to independence, but rather on their growth to self-knowing. In societal terms, I became grown up at a very young age, because that was what I believed gave me love. But I don't think I had my journey of coming of age until these last two years when I got quiet and still and met the small child; I watched on those mental movie reels sit alone and I sat beside her, say, *Hello, I'm here and I'm never going anywhere.*

My coming of age was that meeting between my true self and the manufactured one. Now we walk together, growing and molding, and holding hands.

Affirmation: *I stay close with my inner child, acknowledging the journey so far.*

What Does My Body Need?

The easy answer is to be cared for and to be given attention.

Part of my held stress is from long ago, when I was no longer cared for. I was taught how to do it myself and how to do it for others, and that gave me power and independence. It also gave me praise. All those things felt good—I can help others! I'm good at it! I want to be a mom and do it for a living I'm so good at it.

But what happened?

I locked up my little self and never let her out. I said, "I'm all grown up now. You don't need to be cared for. I've got this." Now, I'm breaking down the walls in the only way she knows how: through my body. It's because my mind is too smart and my heart too focused on everyone else.

This tradeoff between my body's needs was what put me in the hospital in the first place. It opened the flood gate. Feeling is triggered by thought but lives in the body, and the body has a purely natural way to communicate its needs, way better than our sophisticated brain tries to handle things.

I wonder, where does the third element, spirit, or soul come into the picture? Is this the *something* larger?

The planning, goal-setting, monitoring, analyzing, problem-solving— all the mind's job. But what if we divided up the tasks for all three? What if we gave the body some of it? And the soul? But we can't do that without first providing each element with what it needs.

What does the brain need?
- o   Goals; connections; nourishment; rest; opportunities to work

What does the body need?
- o   Good food, nourishment; less stress; sleep and rest to rejuvenate.

What does the soul need?
- o   Meaning, connection, love, simplicity.

All three—brain, body, soul—might need similar things, but how they are fulfilled might be different.

Affirmation: *My body has the answers my mind is seeking.*

Living the Struggle

I've been staying with this *aching* that is created the minute my mind says, "You don't deserve a break! Why are you better than anyone else to get off the merry-go-round for a bit and pause? Who gave you the right to stop what you're doing—quitter?"

The work is so deeply-rooted to trauma. I need to accept that it doesn't need to be justified, it just is. My body and soul have a very large need that I've been neglecting and it doesn't really matter why or when, just that I need to focus on that need, stop the bleeding and heal.

Victory doesn't come from the achievement or persevering through the struggle. Victory is *living the struggle,* embracing the pain. How would it feel for someone in paralyzing grief to have someone else sit by their side and say:

"This is your beauty, right now. You are pure light."

Affirmation: *I am pure light.*

Societal Expectations

My struggle is twofold: Am I still just an adolescent trying to test the boundaries because I was never given any? Or is there truly some awakening I can have and provide the story to give others the freedom to try?

I want to live a life where I can feel all my emotions, live through them *and* listen to my body and spirit during the process. I've been getting input from those who love me and 'healthcare experts' who immediately ask, have you tried a low dose of anxiety meds? I get a visceral defensive reaction.

Don't they get it?

I've been masking these emotions my whole life to try and conform and meet the expectations of family and society and look what it's given me? I have my body screaming at me to listen and I'm just going to quiet it with a pill? I'm actually feeling more and more rage with the thought of this—it's like the little girl who's been locked away has broken free, I've grabbed her hand and we are starting to walk together and she has strength I've never felt before.

She is saying, don't you *dare lock* me up again! I want to learn from the process; I want to feel and flow and fail and get up again. I want that freedom. It seems our current standards do not allow this. If I should fall out of line—I visualize school children lined up walking together—or if I should stop on a rock for a rest, I am scolded. *GET UP!* Join the rest of the line, get back in line, continue achieving and being what the society/family expects of you.

I don't want to stay in line. I want to be free. I want to create. I want to support others who need to sit on a rock. This is my calling. Breaking free of this conformity, allowing myself and others to actually take care of themselves and that sometimes means hitting a massive pause button.

Why do we call life a grind? Is that good? Is that joyful?

What parts of someone's life do they reflect on with honor and love? I'm thinking it's not the daily grind. I'm thinking it's the smile you gave that seemed to touch someone in a way you didn't expect. I'm thinking it's the joy you see from your children's laughter. I'm thinking it's the struggle you work through and support others through just being by their side. This is the purpose of life.

Affirmation: *Today, I try something new to ignite a spark of breaking free.*

What I Asked My Mother:

"Mom," I say, *"Do you remember the day when my friend was over, and we were acting really goofy, and you said, 'What's gotten into you? You are not being yourself?'*

In hindsight, *I wished* I'd said, *No, this is the real me!*

These days I crave silence, being alone, no socializing needed. I'm wondering if that's me just going back to my childhood roots, when I was told that being goofy wasn't 'me.'

I want to ask her about belonging.

Do we feel a certainty of belonging until our eyes are open to others? And in the quest to be less self-centered and grow into a good community citizen does our hope for belonging shift from being within to being external? I guess the unique quality of humans versus other species is our need for connection and community. But how large a net does this really need to be? Once we see the light shone on the bigger society we live within, are we subject to judgment if we do not live within the expectations and boundaries of said society?

Perhaps a hundred years ago, when the light could only be cast as far as the candle shone, the attempt for belonging stayed at home, within the family and oneself. Now we are given the enormous spotlight of being able to see the world and the attempt to *belong* becomes almost impossible—or at least polarizing between different philosophical camps.

What if we take more time to ensure we feel right in our own skin, and start first by ensuring we belong to ourselves. What would that look like? Would we find ourselves belonging, right now, without anyone's input?

Then the circle to which we choose to share our light will not judge, but honor us for all the imperfections we cast in our shadows.

Affirmation: *I belong.*

Bath for Breakfast

My bath is my perfect 'being' place. It checks the box of my productive-self, saying, 'Are you doing something?' To which I respond, "why, yes, I'm taking a bath!" And then I've given myself permission to just be myself and relax.

The bath has become one of the only places in my house where I feel like I can completely focus on taking care of myself. I can read, or stare, or think, or rest, or text, or write—whatever it is, is just exactly what it needs to be.

I recognize that this is different for each one of us, as unique as we are as beings.

For some, it could be a walk in the woods, a run on gravel, listening to music, or cleaning even. I believe what's important is finding out for yourself what that perfect place is and being okay to honor it, not sacrifice it—even if it means taking a bath in the morning after breakfast!

There is also an aspect of awareness to what calls you. For me, it's definitely the water: ocean, lake, river, waterfall, any will do the trick. My bath brings those home to me. This doesn't mean a walk in the woods, with the earth and fresh air doesn't also fill me up, but at my core water is my balancer. I guess it's because I have the fire of a Scorpio so I seek something to let my soul flow.

Find your place to be and don't let go.

Affirmation: *I find my place to be and bathe in it!*

Failure (Part One)

Today is one of those days where I feel like a fish being flushed down the failure toilet. The water (or inner script) keeps spinning round and round, lower and lower with the mantra 'failure' as the sewer drain. I'm flapping my tail and trying to use my gills to hold onto the sides and not go completely dark, but it's more work than I have the energy for. The inner script is amazingly strong sometimes. My top hits include:

- o You're failing as a mother and are running out of time.
- o You are imposing more hurt than love with your kiddos.
- o You are out of your league; who do you think you are?
- o You failed as a wife, as a mother, and now as an entrepreneur.

I haven't quite learned the gift of perspective. In the moment it shifts, when I stop and give in, letting the toilet drain, the darkness is encompassing but survivable. I give into the fear, let it run through me—typically in long, breathtaking cries—and I come out the other side. Nothing has changed, all the doubts could still be doubts; all the actions that lead to running the script are done anyway, just as they were already. But my body has processed it and with that, comes some relief, some peace, some shift.

We all have to use the toilet, so maybe trying so hard to resist the inner script shouldn't be the goal, but rather letting it run its full recording, letting the body flush it out, so the hunger for hope and positivity can rise.

Failure (Part Two)

I was raised as the 'perfect little girl,' which might seem like the ultimate praise; however, it ends up being a burden because no one is perfect, though, I certainly felt I needed to be at all times.

Not much room for failure in that model.

Flash-forward to my parenting, which for me has been the ultimate learning ground for my upbringing. I find myself triggered whenever my son isn't getting straight A's. Now I know it's great to motivate and support a smart gifted child to do their best, and knowing their best *can* be an 'A.' Here's the problem with the model: life gets in the way.

My son struggles with all sorts of social anxiety, living in the black and white world of autism. He's completely capable of getting an 'A,' but he's also equally capable of getting an 'F!' But my perfect little girl syndrome is way too scared to tolerate those Fs. Instead of using those times as opportunities for growth, I get triggered and the fear takes over.

It's said that the first step to overcoming something is admitting you have a problem. So, I recognize this little girl, I say, 'hello,' and when I'm in a good place, I'm even capable of consoling her and telling her everything is going to be okay. This entire internal healing takes time and all the while, my son is sitting there wondering what the heck just happened to his mom and wonders how important it really is to get the 'A.'

Here's the revelation: the perfection is only expected on things *I deem* important. If he got a 'C' in art, it wasn't as critical as if it was a primary class. But what kind of message am I sending? Grades are important. Sure. Not being triggered, imperative. Just being... priceless.

Affirmation: *I shift my perspective of failure to one of gratitude for its lessons.*

Suck Up the 'Suck'

Our life paths change. The work I set out to do in the mainstream didn't fall into place. As a result, it's left me heartbroken because I gave myself somewhat of an ultimatum that if this didn't work out it was the final straw, that this type of career life is just not for me. Left feeling stuck, and with the burden of financial responsibility, I've set off into a new realm of opportunities and growth. It means surrendering fear and following my entrepreneurial spirit. With this leap of faith comes great risk.

Even during great risk, we have to put a stake in the ground. It may take sludging through the difficulties, but at the same time, I plan to focus my energy towards my journey. I don't know how—only that I'm going to do it. And it's not because I'm habitually a perfectionist and over-achiever driven to succeed—those are actually my gifts and talents and the way I thrive—but it's that I trust myself to try. I have created a plan and took one step, then another on the path of my true calling. I don't need to know the *exact* destination as long as I look down daily and know I'm on the path—I'm living it!

Before I attain complete success in my new chapter, I will consciously agree to 'suck up the suck' and continue with my daily grind. Some days are harder than others to continue living a path in parallel with my journey to inner light. I won't let that stop me – I will charge forward and move one foot in front of the next.

Affirmation: *I trust myself to try.*

Unspoken Words

I grew up without conflict. At least that's how it seems my memory serves. I never learned how to deal with it, how to handle anger or sadness or disappointment. But now when I meditate and sit with my inner self, I can see there was conflict abounded. There was anger, and sadness and disappointment, it just wasn't spoken. I learned all the cues from body language and tone. My intuition was peaked to be on watch. Once I sensed the shift, my walls went up, I stayed inside my fortress.

Today, I hear the tone used when my hubby says, "Nope." My visceral reaction is astounding. My little self is busy, quickly stacking the bricks I've spent so much time demolishing. *Please stop building. Please. Sit with me. You sense anger? You sense disappointment? It's going to be okay. It doesn't mean you aren't loved. These are not your emotions to carry. Put down the bricks.*

I'm trying to learn. To build *a pause* instead of a wall. Through unspoken words so much trauma is uncovered. I'm trying to let it out, let it breathe, and then let it wash away in the rain of my tears.

Affirmation: *I trust my intuition to guide me.*

I Am a Woman Who....

I am a woman who...

Feels like a girl

Likes it quiet

Appreciates all of Earth's elements

Needs her friends

Would dance and sing in the rain in a heartbeat

Is defined by her family but is trying to know her own identity

Cries after an orgasm

Is flawed just like everyone else and trying to accept it

Finds power in knowledge

Could sit by the ocean for a lifetime

Deeply desires to spread love but is trying to figure out how to grow it
within herself

The Metaphoric Tea

My life is not linear—and for that, I feel shame.

The *shoulds* of society's expectations are pushed against my psyche every day. The order of progress towards a goal. Then select another goal and make progress towards that. I've always achieved my goals, because that is what was expected of me and that is what made me feel loved, meeting the expectations of others. But I'm not sure I ever figured out what my inner voice had to say. I put her in a room and closed the door, without looking back. Now she's gotten loud enough banging on the walls and door and breaking free, but all her unheard screaming has made her voice go numb. She wants to tell me, but I have to heal her voice.

Let out of the locked room, we sit together and try to heal.

Metaphorically drinking tea, I soothe her throat so she can speak the truth within me. I have to be patient. I have to be kind. Mostly, I have to show her she's not alone and I am here, and that I'm not going anywhere. I can feel anxious in anticipation of what she has to say, but I have to trust when she is ready her voice will be heard.

She is a girl with fiery passion, deeply intense emotions, that is afraid to share them.

I am here, I say, it's ok.

Affirmation: *I sit with my inner child and listen to her story.*

Rebirth: The Lifestyle of a Juggler

The day started like any other. Chaos of kids and parents getting ready. Kids indistinguishable to the likeness of zombies, grunts, slithering bodies, flopping down. Parents moving about like very wise honeybees, knowing just the right places to strike the flower for maximum pollen: in and out of the kitchen; in and out of the bathroom; making breakfasts; making lunches; doing makeup; doing hair. Chaotic by any observer but resonating with a lower frequency of order and routine that only my family can hear.

Traveling the short, but crowded journey into work to find the closest parking spot for safety, time, and efficiency. Hustling into work to make the first morning meeting or conference call, but pausing right before it starts to inhale—*Is this it? Is this my life?* Get out of the car, lock it, exhale, and let the hustle begin.

All normal for the lifestyle of a juggler.

But this day was *different*—that pause was made, because of a retreat I took the prior weekend. A simple getaway for two days in the Berkshires, alone—yes, that's right, alone... who knew being alone with the universe granting you space, time, nature and access to connection and growth, could be so life-changing in just two days.

I certainly didn't know it. I knew the weekend felt amazing, and was just what I needed: a recharge, refresh, then back to reality with a full battery-charge to take on the world. But it wasn't that. That was just a veil I put upon it. Something was stirring inside me, something had been awakened, and was about to make a lot of noise.

The first sign was the pause in the parking lot, the questioning. It wasn't a new question, that sort of existential questioning has always been a pastime or hobby for me. But as I said, that was just the first sign.

The inner being that arose was not going to be quiet for long—like a newborn right before the first breath—all others holding theirs, waiting for the sweet sound of the baby's cry. But I wasn't pregnant. No baby in sight. Who knew your body could create a rebirth without you being truly aware? Could I say to the world, "I swear I didn't know I was going through a transformation and pain is the price of entry?"

In a short time, the woman is awakened and gave birth to a new journey and new future. It was the moment of stepping into the light.

Affirmation: *I am open and ready for all the good that will come.*

Another Decade

My first decade started in the 1970s and bridged the 1980s and was filled with joy, optimism, childhood dreams, magic and wonder.

My second decade bridged the '90s and was filled with ambition, independence, a girl becoming an adult woman warrior. No fear, only hope and goals and dreams.

My third decade brought me achievement. My goals of my master's degree, marriage, and children were all realized. I felt like I had it all, and could do anything and everything.

My fourth decade has been my reality wake up call. I had been in the clouds my whole life, asleep, but then this decade brought me down to earth. The pain of the fall was life-changing.

This past decade, I learned to embrace the earth, the reality of life's messiness, its imperfection, and learn to love myself just a little more.

Each decade has regretless memories, tokens of life-lessons, laughter, and tears that have expanded who I am even beyond my childhood wonder could have imagined.

I walk into this next decade embracing the joyful childhood spirit I might have lost, holding hands with the grounded-woman I've become, and looking up to the light of the sun, knowing each day will bring unexpected twists and turns, all of which I will embrace and let flow. I can't wait!

Affirmation: *I cultivate peace and joy all around.*

Imagine a Place

Do I have a dream?

I'm getting confused. I go from reading about self-healing, to books on self-ownership and self-motivation and I'm feeling stuck. In the room of my life dreams, I walk up the metaphorical staircase to reach my dream and realize, I was actually walking downstairs. I'm turned around. At the crux of my confusion is this conundrum, I believe my heart, mind and soul are all aligned to a life purpose of being a mother, caring wholeheartedly for my children with everything they need. Can this be it, the one purpose? Or have I been living a jaded view of what a dream is? Defined by others all this time, and missing it?

I've come to realize we have *plenty* of great ideas, but only one that truly sits in our heart, guiding our dream. *Ugh! So what the heck?* If that's true, then are my pursuits in starting a wellness retreat a dream or just an idea? Can I own my dream of being a mother with another dream that is just *mine*? My biggest conundrum: unlike those who have this burning desire towards their ambitious, career-driven dreams and feel guilty leaving children aside sometimes, I love being a stay-at-home-mom. My career dream is one I want to put up boundaries around so as not to conflict with the stay-at-home dream. Can I have both?

It will take going enough of the way in to be self-fulfilled, while still allowing the time and energy I want to give to my family. You could say I'm going to have my cake and eat it too. And what's wrong with that?

Affirmation: *My dream will become reality, as long as I keep checking in with myself.*

Silent Prayers

My mother once said, "I found myself still with my prayer hands together when I woke the next morning." I thought to myself, my mother prays every night? I vaguely remember this ritual when we were young, but it was mostly a nursery-rhyme-style prayer that became unconscious as I spoke.

A few days later, while listening to the ramblings of my mother in law, she said, "I touch the statue Mary while I say my evening prayers." Wait a minute? She prays too?

I had to laugh at myself. I find fulfillment in learning and discovering, even if it's knowledge of others and not new information. Lately, I've been focusing my exploration on wholesome living, mindful living. Meaningful living. What I keep stumbling on is the western culture trying to catch up with the eastern traditions when it comes to collective harmony and mindfulness. The act of meditation is spreading like wildfire; books and articles on science and research are being spun up constantly with new topics and potentials around every angle possible, helping us to understand.

But what's different about prayer than some of the guided meditations to send love to yourself and others? Why are we acting as if this is new? I mean, we know it's not new in eastern culture, and there is a subculture of westerners who have practiced meditation for decades, but what about prayer?

As much as we try to blaze our own trails through life, separate from our parents, some things are more the same than we care to see.

Affirmation: *I am grateful for all the traditions I've been exposed to.*

Chameleon

Some people, like me, know how to adjust to different environments, gather different tools along the way and use what's necessary in the moment. It can be very tiring and if not allowed to be whatever the natural color is, could risk total breakdown.

Others are really good at ONE color. They've built their life successes and comfort on this. But their environment is changing and it feels scary and uncomfortable.

How do we still accept their uniqueness in the changing environment?

Affirmation: *Change is hard. I trust the process.*

A Little Patience...

Times I can remember being taught patience with work or life purpose. First career, not liking what I was doing and talking with my dad about wanting to quit and him advising to *wait* until I was fully vested in my pension. It was so hard to see the forest through the trees. I remember thinking, *that's three months away, I couldn't possibly wait!*

Started out during pregnancy, the first feeling of being taught patience. I was uncomfortable, feeling ill most of the first pregnancy and just wanting *to start* being a mom, to realize how much fun it can be to be pregnant and how the anticipation itself brings joy to people.

Now it's every day, having my patience tested.

It doesn't feel like a lesson as much as a test. But maybe those are the same thing? Asking my children—no joke—seven times to come to the table for food, or clear their plates, or brush their teeth, or get their shoes on, or come help me with something. Anything I ask of them requires the queen of patience to wait for it to actually be realized.

What am I doing wrong with this?

I want obedience.

I want compliance.

I want ease.

Those things are nonexistent in my house. Maybe that's my need for control. Is learning to be patient actually linked to learning how to let go of control? If we don't have a set of expectations, and things we want to

135

be a certain way, then we can't feel cast into desperation when they don't go that way.

Every day I feel my patience is tested because I have set expectations that do not get met and launch my discomfort in not being able to control outcomes. Where do I hang my hat if not in the world of trying to control it? It's not too easy to just tell a person, who needs control, to stop.
Maybe it's as simple as starting with one step. Like people who get frustrated trying to quit a habit, like smoking. There are those who quit cold-turkey, but most do better by starting out with the fancy gum or using the patch. Slowly, they start to live life without it and realize there is a new life emerging.

The key is that patience comes from self-compassion, when we care for ourselves in the 'right' way, slowly being less critical of ourselves or those around us.

Affirmation: *I put my wants aside and let life's flow take over.*

Mind Over Matter

I find myself dwelling on the loss of a distant friend. I only met her a few times, but the fact is, she was young, healthy, beautiful, appeared happy and a new mother.

I keep feeling this lost-feeling like there is something I've missed and this event has made me hypersensitive to my health and what could be lying dormant and causing chaos.

Could the stress that I've allowed into my body manifest as illness sneaking up on me?

I'm a full believer that another friend, who survived cancer, did so because of her attack of positivity and change in life-pursuits. She stopped working crap jobs that made her stressed and started focusing on herself.

What will it take for me to do the same?

Affirmation: *I focus on what is good in my life and let that drive my purpose.*

Parking Lots

Does anyone else leave the house and drive to random parking lots just to be away? Not wanting to actually be in public with anyone else, rather being as alone as possible.

Quiet...

I find it fascinating that I would have always described myself as an extrovert, since I'm very social, easy to talk to, good at keeping conversation bouncing between people, the facilitator at heart. But when I think about what I need to recharge and refuel, it's this: being away from people, in nature, or by the water is ideal.

I almost need to reset my balance by the elements. But this is where my guilt lives. My human giver-syndrome chimes in. *Why are you abandoning the kids? They need you. What makes you think it's okay to sit in quiet away from people, you should be acting the way that's expected of you.*

What if what's expected of me is this: me sitting beside a quiet stream, alone, just being?

Affirmation: *It's okay to do what is necessary for yourself, first.*

Birthday Candles

I recently learned that a very close friend of mine, the most selfless woman I know, allows herself *selfish* birthday wishes. I don't know why it struck me as so alarming, that a woman who spends her life giving everything of herself to all of those she loves and even to strangers, would make wishes for herself.

Once a year, in her giver-soul of upbringing, she grants permission to have this one indulgence, and for it to be okay.

Here's the thing: it really need not be once a year. There is a way for the people-givers of the world to turn a mirror on themselves and do some of that awesome giving for themself, each and every day.

And it's not called being selfish, it's being human.

It's not over-indulgent to give to yourself each day, it's sane.

If I had the magic-wand I would grant this permission to all of us.

Make a wish every day and then go live it.

Affirmation: *I start every day with a wish.*

Hide and Seek

Maybe the universe presents opportunities throughout our lives to help us find ourselves. Lucky or not, some have it easy, which I could hypothesize are the ones who grew up tough, the ones who have real-life from an early age. Working hard through manual labor, taking care of younger siblings, or simply being brought up with clear communication about their family values and beliefs. *Hmm...* but even then, the minute we enter into our family unit, whatever it may be, we strive to fit in—isn't it rare for the child to be unique and different from the family norm—how long do they keep their unique identity solid?

If life is one long journey of hide-and-seek for our inner truth, it makes sense how obstacles are cast upon us as that little nudge (e.g., *warmer, warmer ... oh colder, colder... COLD! No, hot!*) to find the inner child who might be hiding.

The hardest part is to pause and see that these shifts, the twists and turns, are gifts, clues to help in the hunt. It's hard to trust that inner, intuitive voice. It's so quiet and it seems like it's leading us into a really dark room, one we don't have control over. We can't turn on the light. Who would want to enter that room? But think about it. Isn't that exactly the best place to hide? In the game of life's hide and seek, it's in the darkest closets and nooks that you are found.

So I say, give that little voice a try, take a few steps into the room. You don't need to know where or why, just step inside and be still. If you are really quiet, you might hear your calling rise up a little louder as it's getting tired of hiding and wants to be found.

Affirmation: *I know that if I'm uncomfortable, it means I'm growing.*

Just Know

Just know...

It's all okay.
You will feel everything. Then you will feel nothing.
You will feel regretful, guilty, relief, heavy, light, sorrow, hope, love.

Just know...

It's all okay.
Some days will be like moving through mud.
Then some will be dizzying and groundless.

Just know...

It's all okay.
Friends and family will reach out; you won't have the courage, energy,
motivation to respond.
Then you'll feel alone and yearn to connect with the ones you love.

Just know...

It's all okay.
You will think you could have done more.
Then you will think you had a good life together and the time had come.

Just know...

It's all okay.
You are loved.
Everything that flows through you, is loved too.

Calling

Joy that makes you cry.

Tightness in the stomach that makes you curl over a bit.

All in awe that something so simple could feel so good.

So, I've found it, writing, you are my creative soul mate. I found you late. I must have met you before, because I remember our first date, the incessant need to put fingers to keys, to create a story, tell a story through written words. I think that was 7th or 8th grade. I guess you were my first love, but I was blind to the knowing, my filter only allowed boys to be considered.

But you, my love, are it, the true first love. I'm so happy we have reunited. Please don't go far, because as you know, I'm still working on abandonment issues (nudge, nudge). You fill my soul, heart, mind and body.

Oh, and you are part of me, allowing me to love myself completely, in wholeness.

Journal Exercises: The Inner Child

I found many guided meditations on the inner child. Ways to connect with your childhood self. Much of my writing stems from those meditations.

Please use these journal exercises to allow the time and space to connect with your inner child.

1. Are you really as grown up as you think? Or just by the world's definition? What's your definition? I urge you to ask your little one. (Ref: A Happy Grown-Up; Coming of Age).
2. Write down aspects of yourself that might feel neglected. Reflect on difficult experiences and let the struggle unfold through your words. Allow this to be your beauty. (Ref: Living with Struggle; Being Heard).
3. What truth can you uncover about your childhood that you may be craving to return to today? (Ref: What I Asked My Mother; The Little Girl).
4. What is your deep intense emotion that you're afraid to share? (Ref: The Metaphoric Tea; Hide and Seek).
5. Are you a chameleon with many colors or deeply rooted in one rich, vibrant one? How does this aspect of you help/hinder your ability to flow with change? (Ref: Chameleon; Societal Expectations).
6. Spend time writing all the aspects of life that bring you joy—
    From when you were a child through to today. How can you ensure you keep this joy alive? (Ref: Calling; Just Know).

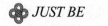

AWAKENING

Lucky 7s

"It was a long road to get to where you are so it'll take some time to get to where you want to be."

I'm driving down the road, taking time for my life through ways I know will help my mind, body and soul. I'm on my way back from driving to the water—the element that will always fill me back up. I'm thinking about the cycle of seven and how pertinent it is to my changes.

It's been seven years since my divorce. It took seven years to grieve—I may have been in a seven-year tunnel, really! It doesn't mean it's been all doom and gloom and darkness at every turn. I've had my friends and loved ones right beside me to go through the tunnel together. I've had moments of amazing empowerment, hope and joy. But I wasn't *all the way* through yet when those moments happened.

It brings me to the time I gave myself one weekend, not seven— basically 72 hours, just for me. No one else. No friends. No loved ones, just me. I gave myself exactly what I needed—space, rest, nature, time, yoga, reflection and a community of strangers feeling the same tugs.

So that's awesome right?! Yay me! Who gets a chance to have 72 hours all to themselves when we become adults with responsibilities, families and work to take care of. I should feel rejuvenated and grateful and re-energized to continue my path, right?

Here's what happened—I ended up in the emergency room. Yup, I came back from my weekend and had all these refreshing ideas, approaches to fulfill and then the kids came home. And then I drove into work, and then lunchboxes were being made, and sports were being coordinated and the wheel just kept spinning 'round and 'round.

And I ended up in the ER. It sounds more dire than it was, but maybe that's still my ego trying to resist moving aside and letting me take care of me. I woke up on about the fourth day and had pain in my chest. I had tingling in my hands and felt a shortness of breath and lightheaded. Well, I wasn't going to let that get in the way of what I'm *supposed* to do, so I continued on, because I was taught to be strong and persist.

My body didn't say much more than that. It just didn't stop. And my soul stepped in and opened up my mind and said, "Hello? What are you doing? Why are you ignoring me?" Friends were suddenly concerned. Nothing turned up. EKG fine, bloodwork fine, chest x-ray fine. But my body knew otherwise.

My mind was saying, "Would you rather wait until you *do* have a heart attack to take action or just be given this nudge?"

We need more than 72 hours to reach the kind of level of real self-exploration that will heal. Truth be told, my body has been talking to me, but I just haven't been listening. It's always saying something in my neck and shoulders, and every so often my lower back throws out to *have mercy!* Giving myself those 72 hours, was not only my final stop in the tunnel, but it afforded me a view of the light at the end of it. In actuality, I could *finally* feel it! The warmth and peace it feels to love yourself and take care of yourself. But I was also deprived—we have to know one in order to recognize the other.

We get *very* used to living inside the tunnel. We accept the suffering, over finding the light inside us. I got out, the moment I started to listen to my body to guide me to what my soul needed.
I haven't looked back since.

Affirmation: *I listen to my body to guide me to what my soul needs.*

Winning Yourself Back

We often grow up reading articles about how to succeed at love or how to reach our dreams, but in the midst of actually living life, we might wake up one day and see we 'lost' ourselves following what others deem the 'best way' to have the things we want. Amongst the tears, sweat and sleep, of my self-awareness, I'm finding it helpful to capture concrete ideas about navigating this nebulous, ambiguous journey.

1. Research your soul fillers: Find the things you love, like running, cooking, being with friends, yoga, meditation etc., and take some time reflecting on when you felt the most joy, the most filled and jot it down. Do more of what you love and allow it to support your life.

2. Make a wish list: It's time to write down the best of the best of the things you want in life. Don't constrain yourself with not having time or money. Wish and dream. Make a list and see what's possible.

3. Talk to family/spouse about your wish list—your needs—and how they can help you take a step towards fulfilling at least one. This is a must. Look at your list together and start to have a conversation about what could really be doable.

4. Declare your SELF-CARE Rules: If you run a household full of rules, clear your plate, so to speak, make your bed, clean up your room, be kind to each other, and then create your self-care rules that *you* have to follow. Start where it feels doable.

5. Enlist self-care advocates. As much as we want to be able to rely *only* on ourselves to be accountable, it's hard and having a support system to cheer you along, without judgments, can actually ensure your success. Take time each day to check in with your self-care advocates, to let them know you're following your rules.

6. Don't beat yourself up: Any new activity can cause difficulty and be tough to start and then stick with. So don't beat yourself up and allow for the unexpected. Try to look at it as a way to learn more about yourself, make tweaks to the plan as you need, breathe and flow through.

Now go get yourself back. Joy and wholeness are waiting for you.

Affirmation: *I have a plan towards self-care and I will honor it.*

Excuse Me! Emotional Neglect is My Business.

There is a parallel between relationships with someone who has had emotional neglect in their past and one of running a business during a pandemic—or should I say *opening* a business during a pandemic. *(Who thought that was a good idea?)*

Here are the parallels:

In a relationship we say:
"Maybe I should wear that low-cut dress and get my hair done. I think he'll like that."

Opening a business, we say:
"Maybe I'll show behind the scenes and all the beautiful features of the space. I think they'll like that."

In a relationship we say:
"I hope he calls! I hope he calls! I think he likes me! I think he likes me!"

Opening a business, we say:
"I hope they book! I hope they book! I think they'll like it! I think they'll like it!"

In a relationship we say:
"I am worthy of love."

Opening a business, we say:
"I am worthy of love."

My emotions are low when the business is slow. My emotions rise when the business rises. I watch. I consider. I need to be careful.

I am awakened now, which in laymen's terms just means *aware*. It doesn't necessarily mean I know what to do with what I see.

So, I watch.

I observe.

I see.

The parallel is obvious to me.

Now what to do?

Pause... definitely pause...

That is what I've learned.

Pause...be still...and wait...

There is more to learn.

There is more to grow.

I am honored to see my path still winds ahead of me. And taking time to love myself is key.

Have you found your key?

Affirmation: *I am worthy of love.*

The Hoax of Comparison

Past meets the present—everything I need to heal from as a child shows up every day as a parent.

I'm stuck finding myself comparing my stress and emotions to others. The minute I look at others and compare my struggles it devalues my feelings. Even in the hopes to maintain positivity, we are told to look at different perspectives because others definitely *have it worse.*

How do I get out of the game? The game of comparisons.

The victim shows up pretty easily during this game. Her gameplay rules show up as whispers:

They don't have kids who meltdown every day after school.
– Score 1 for you!

They aren't trying to hang on to the last thread of order through the chaos that is the end of the day or school year.
– Score 2 for you!

They don't know what success feels like to simply have joy show up in their household, because it's such an infrequent visitor.
– Score 3 for you!

Playing this game can be addictive if left alone. I find myself wanting to *win* the 'Who's got the crappier life?' game.

What sort of insanity is that?

I remind myself: comparison comes with no good end. It's only played in the shadows. I've learned to move into the light and put my game chips down.

Affirmation: *I move away from comparison into the light of compassion.*

What I'm Meant to Be Doing?

Answer: teaching.

And then I bawl.

It seems so simple. Why does it seem so difficult? My inner voice screams—hello? You've known this since you were six and loved getting a chalkboard for the holiday. You want to talk to masses and have your words resonate, make impact, ignite a sudden shift inside others. It's been your yearning.

What am I meant to be doing? Those words have planted seeds of new ways of thinking, feeling, being. I'm just the planter though. Just the provider of seeds. That's enough. I add value by planting the seed.

Affirmation: *Today, I look within to find answers to what I'm meant to be.*

Politics

Everyone has struggles. No one is granted a free pass from that. It's the ones who lay blind to their struggles, who cast criticism towards others' differences in order to avoid their own. What we need is more compassion.

More apologies.

More acceptance.

Because we are all human, no matter what color our skin, what gender we do or don't identify as, who we love, what interests we have, what special needs we have.

We are all human beings who need love and acceptance to make this world a better place.

Affirmation: *I forgive and accept humanity and offer to it my compassion.*

Connection

I just spent what felt like a few minutes (if measured by progress) but was actually a couple hours in the world of social media. All I wanted to do was get connected with like-minded spirits who could embrace the mess with me together. As I stretched out of my chair and looked around my room, I couldn't help but think, "Wow, it's sunny out, what time is it?"

It's left me feeling somewhat numb, a zombie-like glaze in my eyes from the screen, and I wonder does this really connect us more? Maybe it's because my voice on social media is only one-sided right now; I haven't actually joined in the conversation yet.

Maybe once I feel the spark of discussion based on my writing, I'll feel the familiar tug of connectedness in my heart that I believe we all seek.

I know it will take time, that nothing is as easy as it seems. I have to curb my inner teenager who is demanding instant gratification and let her know—*All good will come in time, breathe deep, what's meant to be will come.*

Affirmation: *What's meant to be will come.*

Let's Do the Hokey Pokey

My stomach has decided to be the house of stress this week. Sometimes it's my neck and shoulders. Sometimes my lower back. Sometimes it's my knees and other joints. There are medical reasons that doctors will tell me cause the pain—Lyme's Disease; inflamed discs; not wearing the right shoes or sleeping the right way. I know that although those might be some of the reasons for the pain, it truly is my body's way to hold the stress and decide what it's going to do with it.

It's like my body says, *hmm, should we tell her about this or can we handle it?* Yup, this one we better bring to her attention.

So the stress goes from head to toe and plays the hokey-pokey through my system. If there is one thing I've learned, it's that I need to stop and listen. Give the space and pause to connect with my body and ask, *what's up? Are you ok? How can I help?* Then wait and listen some more for my path to unfold.

Grant yourself this pause. Consult with yourself first, before going elsewhere. You hold a wisdom that only you can tap into.

Affirmation: *My body is a vessel of knowledge I trust.*

To Be or To Change

In order to *be,* does that mean we don't change? And if we are changing, does that mean we're not simply being?

I find myself drawn to anything that promotes transformation, growth, deeper understanding, awakening, or sits on the foundation that change is our only constant. What I'm struck with is this question:

Can my quest for transformation also live in the same space as just being?

Is the journey to transformation actually through the door of self-being? Is there a struggle between doing and being or is it just the balance of the two that can promote transformation?

My change is the shift from doing to being. My change is the acceptance to allow self-care in. My change is being okay with what *is* without any other change needed.

Maybe we all need to take a pause to consider that it's not what we are *doing* that needs to change but how we are *being*.

Affirmation: *I allow for self-care.*

Ripple Healing

No matter what age, what stage in life, it seems we have all become accustomed to speed—aka instant gratification. And we certainly expect it with our health. Sprain an ankle, and oh, I'll be walking in a day or two, right? Bulging discs in the spine, a week max, right? It seems we can't accept that healing can be slow.

Healing is, in fact, our gift to slow down.

We are programmed for acceleration, that is the definition of success: to keep going, persevere. How could slowing down possibly be viewed as good or successful? Our body is certainly screaming for it.

It seems because we are moving too fast, reacting to life's pace, we aren't being proactive with ourselves the way we need to. Enough to slow down.

Breathe, please, before your body fails. Try proactively pausing throughout the day and watch the ripple of healing take place. Your body will thank you.

Affirmation: *I grant micro-pauses throughout my day for me.*

The Stream

We think change requires movement. The transition between. When water freezes, then melts, then boils, then condenses—all the shifts and movements we associate with the change. But perhaps if we can just stay still, through stillness our transformation can happen. We need not negate the need for our body to move to help the growth journey, but rather a reminder that in stillness we too can be growing and transforming. In the stillness, we too can follow along our path.

It feels like I'm skating on thin ice. Some days can be carefree, like when I have time for refreshing walks, doing crafty, creative things, feeling positive about how quarantine has made life slow down and we can throw our arms up to the sky with a smile. Other days we are acutely aware of how thin the ice is, just the pressure of the blade against the ice feels dangerous, our internal voice saying, *Don't push hard. You might fall in deep!*

I've lived with this fear that if I fall, the depth of the darkness will be too much to handle. Some days, the sun can be shining bright, birds chirping, and all I feel is dread that life will never be the same.

Fear is real—even with my friends, we connect sometimes in a socially distant way, reminiscent that fear is present. We talk about the crazy life we are living during the pandemic, but it never feels like we allow each other to go deep. Especially on those Zoom calls with those craving connection—what I crave most are the times when I can lay my most troubled thoughts out to my friends and they are there, just holding my hand or hugging me through my tears. I miss that. I'm sick of crying alone. Somehow this quarantine has allowed many to reflect and recognize how critical it is to take care of yourself, but we've lost the physical human connection to take care of each other. We are trying, sure: we talk, we write, we read the social posts, we feel connected, but

159

nothing will compare to the judgment-free hugs from your most trusted loved ones. I miss those hugs.

What I do know is no one is alone. No matter if I try to hold my hubby's hand to skate or keep my grasp while he sinks, I won't let go either way. Our love is like a universal tether that can weave us together. Maybe instead of viewing it as sinking, we can allow the drop, go deeper than the superficial, like a scuba diver with a tether to the boat, never alone, always supported.

Affirmation: *Until I can hug others, I will hug myself and hold my loved ones close.*

Empty Chairs and Empty Tables

All I want is to help others. To share what I have learned, connect with others on an authentically meaningful way, share and grow. It seems the mission is so positive, it's so needed, Today, I'm stuck acting the victim. My space is empty. No souls are being filled. No connections being made. I'm sad. I'm heavy. This part of the journey is tough. If only I didn't have to worry about the financial burden, if only I could march to the music I hear from my core. If only I could broadcast the song so that it doesn't fall on deaf ears.

My space is empty.

It's hard not to let that make me feel empty.

Maybe I grew too many branches before my trunk was solid enough?

Maybe my flowers aren't blooming because I haven't sunk deep enough into the ground, focusing on the nutrients the earth has to offer?

Affirmation: *I do not let my fears and doubts take hold. I stay hopeful in the strength of my inner music.*

Before COVID-19

I never watched the news.

To be honest, I never really gave it a chance. Through all my years, if I stumbled upon it on the TV, it seemed the story being told was not one I wanted to hear, with topics of murder, politics, natural disasters, economic warnings—all seems full of negativity, anger, hate, ego, sadness. The typical concoction of emotions I try to avoid. So, yeah, I don't watch the news.

But just yesterday something happened when I turned the TV on. It was time for the news and what was on my screen was this: a video reel of a pond, with the birds chirping, wind blowing ripples on the water, and the caption: a moment of peace. It was awesome. Someone in some high-paying news office agreed to put dead-air on the screen, with no advertising, no action, no talking at all, the news was 'Just Be-ing!' I thought, it's finally happening! The mainstream pause button has been hit!

My gut reaction was to write this station immediately and say, 'thank you.' But instead, I just enjoyed it.

Affirmation: *I watch for moments of gratitude throughout my day.*

Building in a Pause

Spring is a positive time, where folks get outside, embrace the sunshine, and make the most of each day. But I have found that with this momentum, we can get caught up in an acceleration that is hard to slow down.

It is also a time we can make new plans for new adventures. Of course, we can go and take time away and rejuvenate, but it doesn't mean that there will be a pause when we return to our fast-paced world. For me, returning from my own getaway/spring retreat, it was almost impossible to bear. In the process, what I learned was how to build in micro-pauses throughout the day to elevate the joy the productivity brings and keep me a little more sane along the way.

This micro-pause can come in many ways, but I've found its best grasped during the "in-betweens." In-betweens happen each day while you are sitting at a red light; standing for a moment longer in the shower; stirring the food on the stove; turning the car off to walk inside; washing your hands; while the kids are arguing for the 100th time—you *can* really find these micro-moments in a million spaces throughout the day. The question is whether you will take the opportunity to pause?

Instead of reaching for the phone to check the latest feed, or text, or the next meeting or commitment, take a pause and just breathe in, to allow the lightning bugs of productivity to slow for just a moment between flickers.

And breathe out. No need to put pressure on yourself. No need to try and meditate if you've never done that before. No need to criticize yourself when a monsoon of to-do lists comes washing through your brain. It's all okay. Let it flow.

Build in the pause and just be the journey!

Affirmation: *I release all pressure to move fast.*

Get the 'Should' Out of Here!

I spend so much of my time focused on what I *should do*, what I *should be*, what my family should be, what my relationships should be, the list can go on... But what if I *chose* to accept the reality that I'm a person who likes to be on time, and if others aren't, that's okay.

This simple gift was planted in my mind from my inner voice: *just accept others for who they are.*

Another voice came and added—*just accept you the way you are.*

And the tears flowed.

I don't think I've ever accepted myself for all my imperfections. Instead, I've been on a lifelong quest to try and live up to the external expectations of perfection to avoid failing. So now that I'm listening to myself more, my inner voice is trying to heal and guide me to the peace I thought I'd find in all my *shoulds*.

Because I am perfect in all my imperfections.

Affirmation: *Today, I let the 'shoulds' fall away.*

The Collective Conundrum

I have a theory about the women like me, the generation of women whose parents started breaking out of their shell. Mothers who told daughters, *even though I could only be a teacher or a secretary you can be ANYTHING.* We had fathers who spent time with their daughters, time on activities that might have once been seen as 'manly,' and today aren't. My fondest memories of my time with my dad was always with some sort of tool in my hand, or butt on the ladder, but that doesn't mean I'd run to do building projects today.

My theory is that we were told we could do/be ANYTHING. How does someone figure out the ONE thing then? We are supposed to siphon through a million different choices and funnel them down to one? Is this why when we get old enough to open our eyes to see ourselves for who we've been raised to be we are lost? We have lived just long enough to finally have real struggle, real pain, real love, real loss and the questioning of life's purpose bubbles to the surface.

We ask: *Is this it?*

Is waking up every morning to pack lunches; make sure homework is done; resolve mini-conflicts about who is wearing what hair-tie and where someone's shoes are; to hop in the car and race to work to deal with other people's problems but never our own; to come home and make dinner; rush around for activities; check homework; resolve/support some social conflict happening at school; pay bills; clean; do laundry; sit like a zombie in front of the TV or phone screen right before going to bed—not really sleeping through the night (because sleep has somehow eluded us since our 30s)—and wake up and do it again; is this what we were meant to do?

Long sigh.

Does this lack of purpose stem from too many choices in childhood?

Could one actually complain that could be a bad thing?

Affirmation: *I say, "Thank You" to all the choices I've had and continue seeking and learning.*

Like an Angel

There are angels among us. They're called *Earth angels,* and can't feel the physical pains that the rest of us feel, including the emotional spectrum, yet their response is to just radiate light, through love.

That's what my life feels like. Could it be that when we are born—although *human,* we feel the whole gamut of emotions and physical pain, forgetting we're beings of light and love, like angels?

Through childhood, we experience more of what it means to be human and it either integrates into our being with oneness or is severed, compartmentalized for survival.

I went through life feeling like an angel for much longer than the 'typical' human, then crashed to Earth when my parents divorced. It didn't stop me from flying again though, and I did, living my life full of joy and light. And then I crashed again, with my own divorce. Instead of living my human life fully integrated with all it had to offer, all emotions positive and negative, I lived in denial. My second 'crash' was the start of my spiritual awakening. It was the moment I could no longer ignore my angelic light.

Affirmation: *I spend time honoring my angelic light that came with creation.*

When Bad is Good

It's important to keep gratitude going even through crappy experiences.

Looking back, it's rather apparent how important struggles were to learn something and growing on my journey. But *during* the struggle, *hmm,* not so much.

It's easy to become the victim, especially if it's something as uncontrollable as the flu. As I nurse myself back to health, I recognize the gratitude I have for the struggles I've come through.

Affirmation: *I am open to ask for what the universe has to offer and recognize the answer might come through a journey of struggle.*

Choose Your Own Adventure

I always liked those *Choose Your Own Adventure* books, popular in the 1980s. As a child, it was an exploration of choices. Just picking one way to go, while having many other different endings was exciting, especially when you found out which one was 'best' and if you got into trouble, figuring out the next path to get somewhere new, more promising. I always wanted to know what *all* the options were before I picked. And maybe that's the way our generation has been raised as women who can have anything.

We have finally been given all the choices that our previous generations didn't have. And we feel a deep sense of obligation to choose the right one. Or any one for that matter. But at least for myself, I know this widening of opportunities, this myriad of doors to open, has left me somewhat paralyzed. I harbor a deep need to be right, the perfect little girl that I was viewed as through my parents' eyes, which is an insurmountable expectation.

So when selecting a path, I sit with these expectations of perfection and worry—what if I don't pick the right one?

This lesson is in the redefining of 'right.'

Affirmation: *Today, I am grateful for the many doors in my life and joyfully select one at a time.*

Morning Mantra

You aren't worth hurting for other people.

Your body is leading you, listen and don't ignore.

Nothing is worth putting other people before yourself. Nothing is more important than your health.

Stop worrying about what people will think and do what's right for you.

If people want to doubt your work ethic or morals based on a decision to take care of yourself, you are not in the right place.

Why are you putting the potential assumptions of others over what you need for yourself?

This is real, you are not faking, your body has taken the lead to grant you the rest you need.

Stop worrying about looking like the woman who always has something going on, and start accepting that you are a woman that always has shit going on.

Own it. Honor it. Allow space for it.

Affirmation: *I put myself first. This is not selfish, but necessary.*

People Pleaser

We are the givers, the people-pleasers, the friends, parents, sons and daughters who help others be the best they can be. We pride ourselves in our ability to give. We've defined ourselves by this infinite well of abundant giving that seems to pour onto others.

I've learned a lot about what it means to be one of this tribe. I've learned how my upbringing molded me, how I came to embrace my power, and most importantly how to direct that power onto myself.

I've spent the last few years struggling to understand the reasons for my lack of well-being, from the physical malfunctions to emotional instability to overall chronic stress.

I view adversity as something I might be granted as having faced. I've had my share of struggles, hardships, lows, downs, but adversity? Is it me?

My life was one long how-to book on handling adversity. Having been raised to think positive, be positive, only positive will come.

This lesson is an interesting one, since it seems more of a teaching on pace than it does on attitude. It's more about how to relinquish control over to the Universe and honor what she wants, over what my ego wants.

Adversity might just be seen as misfortune or distress because of our ego. If we release ourselves to God and the flow, we can view the distress as gifts, tollbooths to keep us slowed down and not let our ego take the wheel.

We know that resistance allows us to acknowledge where we've been and where we're going. But adversity doesn't seem to be sourced by a single individual. It's difficult to point the finger at one entity, because it's universal.

If this is true, how can we blame? How can we become a victim? If we stay open, curious and honest, we can see the sparkle of faith adversity offers.

Have faith that we don't drive the boat, but we take it out for one long, beautiful ride.

Affirmation: *I will meet adversity with eyes open, staying curious to what it has to show.*

On Break?

Have you ever seen a sign at a service station that reads, 'on break,' and they are sitting right there making sure they don't make any eye contact?

It might create a visceral reaction of contempt wondering why they get a break and you don't—or that they decided to take it *right* when you needed help. You might even feel justified in feeling the injustice of it— or it might trigger your sense of 'bad luck,' that the Universe is conspiring against you. But there is a gift in witnessing someone resting, possibly even meditating on a break.

As I'm trying to find balance for self-care and the self-care of others, I'm realizing I need to make some hard rules, boundaries if you will, that I won't let others cross, just like the service worker is entitled to a break. For example, I need twenty minutes between work meetings and the time the kids come home to prepare for the transition. This time is still considered during work hours, in our conventional world. Sounds sort of like an *on break* sign doesn't it? But it's become time needed to fundamentally function. But how do I fulfill this need (not want) when society is hardwired to react that this time is an inconvenience?

I think it takes more than keeping my eyes down and not making eye contact, and hope that no one notices I'm taking time for self-care. It takes openness to inform others that it's okay to do it too.

Maybe the next time you see an 'on break sign,' you'll be the gatekeeper and shoo other people away from bothering the worker, granting them permission to continue.

Affirmation: *Today, I chose self-care by taking a break in my workday.*

Self-Aware

I stumbled into a train of thought, reminiscing about my first dates with my hubby. Early on, he'd told me he was a rock, a good shoulder to lean on, someone stable and steady.

I remember thinking, "Well, that's awesome." It made me feel like he was going to be such an amazing source of safety and stability. In kind, I expressed myself very actively with hand gestures and excitable tones about all my interests and ideas, and how passionate I was about life.

Looking back, I can't help but consider how we portrayed ourselves to each other. How well did we grasp one another—were we being real? Was that really how he saw himself? What about me, was I as passionate about the things as I conveyed? Were we truly self-aware, or just faking it?

Imagine your best friend who you always find joy and glow in her smile, but she always complains about her crooked teeth. Or someone you see every day that you deem beautiful, not just by appearance, but through their acts of kindness and generosity, who silently carries heavy insecurity. Or someone you watch in awe as they get in front of large crowds with ease, but internally they are a sweaty, hot mess. Each one of these people could look in the mirror and criticize their big nose, pointy ears, or insecurity to talk in front of crowds.

We spend so much time seeing ourselves through our worst critic's eyes, how could we possibly display the truth?

If looking in the mirror doesn't give the true reflection of ourselves, how do we see it?

I've found meditation is a good start. Also finding the people who love you to a fault and express that love when you are struggling, haggard, and a mess. That's when you can see your true light reflecting back at you, through their eyes. Most importantly, spending time with your inner child, talking to her, loving her, and listening to all she has to teach you.

My sole success—or *soul* success—came when I let myself know I was okay, that I was in control, and didn't have to get anyone else's opinion. Speaking up for myself is how I discovered my 'true' reflection. When I let go of the fear of criticism or judgment from others, anticipated or real, I got stronger; I let go of the tiredness of being defensive too. That's when my true self can shine.

Affirmation: *I bask in the knowing that all I need is within me to be okay.*

History

We can learn a lot from our own history. We are taught about our world's history, but not always our individual heritage—*how often are we made to look at our own history to learn from?*

I was cast into a journey of reflection the first time I hit real struggle, real heartache. It's one of the beauties of pain, the punch in the face to look within, and back. So I looked back, cataloged my experiences, and viewed them as objects to be inspected, to be flipped on their sides, upside down, and around. Here's what I found every time, a revelation. It's quite astonishing, and I don't think it's because there are such profound things for me to learn, but actually just truth staring at my face. Waiting for me to find—here I am!

When I look back, this amazing uncovering I found, this truth, stares back at me. I shake my head, breathe, then pause.

When you look upon an experience that has happened to you, either it gets amplified in its truth or it gets uncovered. For example, as I think more and more about the times my mother is late to pick me up, my emotions get amplified (my inner child saying, yes, this was very uncomfortable. Very real for you). Then I think about my infatuation with a childhood friend and the emotion that rises is curiosity—was that real? Where did that yearning come from, because of him or lack of something? And the truth rises and the discovery and answer is lack.

I just have to say, our own history is quite informative, I'm going to take the time to learn about my own past so I can continue to grow on my path for my future.

Affirmation: *I trust what my past has to teach me.*

My Dog Taught Me How to Be Present

We had a scare last night with our puppy, Millie. She had some sort of allergic reaction to something and her snout was inflamed and she couldn't stop itching. We gave her Benadryl but then it seemed that it kept her awake and made her tummy upset all night. In the morning we took her to the vet and she had to stay there all day. She's fine, they aren't truly certain what she got into, even if it seems like it's passed.

All day working from home without her made me realize that without her by my side, needing periodic attention, I got sucked into the computer screen with the clock spinning and no recognition of how out of touch with the present moments I was. I've been trying to learn more about mindfulness and meditation, the practice of being present, and up until today, I didn't realize how valuable my puppy was in that lesson.

Millie is like a mindfulness bell, keeping me present and aware of the minutes ticking off. These best friends keep coming through for us in so many ways, I can't imagine a life without her! So next time she barks during a conference call or some deep with thought, I'll have to pause and instead of getting angry, say thank you, Millie, for keeping me present.

Affirmation: *Today, I thank all the living things for keeping me present.*

One Step on Dry Land

One step on dry land and it's like my body made a switch. I felt the *shift*, but chalked it up to the end of vacation blues. The letdown after you come home from vacation, trying desperately, without success, to hold on to the bliss that vacation offered. This was my first seven-day trip without kids since my oldest was born—or twelve years. I'm sure that's what most, who have school-aged kids, would say as well. But the shift I'm talking about is the one that comes when you're back home: you have the laundry; need to mow the lawn; do the grocery shopping—the shift is my body moving from a place of *being* to a place of *doing*. I grew immensely aware of it, maybe because I've yet to crack the code. It's a constant practice to *just be,* on vacation, and also at home and at work and in our everyday world. But it's not impossible.

Affirmation: *I am aware of shifts that happen during the in-between and breathe.*

Balancing Scales

Picture Lady Justice with the balancing weight in her hand. Isn't it constantly in motion, back and forth? One side is usually very light, without many things, and the other side is heavy, with those I care about, the people, places, and experiences, I take pride in nurturing and caring for.

My *Just Be* business is an oasis for people to put down their scale. But ironically through building my business, I've struggled with the balance of being a success and staying true to my intention. This is a real toughie, since my creative, entrepreneurial spirit will spin ideas round and round to try and gain some traction and stability, but the intention will speak—*build it and they will come.* But when?

The world has been flipped upside down and being creative and innovative is the way businesses will stay afloat. Being so new, it's hard to tell how much to balance on the first tightrope we laid out in front of us, or hop down to try another?

And remember, I'm still holding that other scale in my other hand. As you might imagine, some days are just plain hard. Sometimes it's a relief to put the whole thing down. Isn't that why this is happening in the first place? But with all the pieces on the ground, many questions arise: which one do I pick up first? Do all the things matter? How about I just lay in this grass and let the sun shine, *yeah...that's good.*

I do know this: I'm not alone. I don't have to look at all the plates fallen on the ground alone. I don't have to figure out my next step all alone. **And I also don't have to know where I'm going to start moving.** One breath at a time, one moment at a time, with true-intention for honoring yourself and the ones you love. That's the Just Be Journey.

And by the way, Lady Justice is not just holding scales—she's holding a sword! She's going to battle or maybe protecting balance—or protecting her intuition, her true authentic self.

Affirmation: *While balancing the scales of life, I know I am not alone.*

Take Care

It's what we are all trying to do right now, right, take care of each other, ourselves, and just simply take the time to care. It's a beautiful thing, but for many of us who are eternal caregivers we've never quite figured out the recipe for self-care.

Yesterday, my stepfather died. Without thought, I started the motions of *taking care* of my mom. I knew she would not be in a position to do anything. We can say it's in our nature to be caregivers, to step into action to help someone we love in need. I guess that's got to be true, because it was instinctual, completely natural. A small part of me was sitting back observing, waiting to see if the stress would rise, waiting for something to snap inside. I've been down this road before: giving yourself completely to someone else and forgetting how to take care of yourself. I know the warning signs; a part of me was on alert, looking for them.

There isn't a formula for self-care. You can't exercise each day, or drink the right amount of water, or give yourself breaks each day, and always expect to feel cared for. Life isn't *even,* it's in constant changing motion. We can say, up and down, but really, it's more like a kaleidoscope of movement. So our attempt for self-care can't be level either. Sometimes stress, emotions, life, can be so hard that an entire day of doing what you need will not fill you up, and other days (like mine today) you can care for others, with little time for yourself, and feel good about the love you were able to share.

As I wait for my emotional walls to crumble, I'm almost void of emotion (which in itself could be a warning sign), but for now, it's just a moment for me to reflect on this lesson. Like I always say, *the only constant is change,* and I believe the only way to maintain self-care is to have your constant be checking-in with yourself. Today, I feel good that I could be the rock my mother needed to get through her first day as a widow, but I won't use this day to determine my future days' need for self-care.

Affirmation: *When I say 'Take Care,' let it be a reminder to check in with myself and assess exactly what care I need to take.*

Diving Board

As we stand on the edge of the diving board to jump back into normal, I feel more fear than before. I know fear should not guide me but at the same time, it's an interesting emotion to be curious around.

My fear feels powerful this time, like it's my own warning sign, one I've grown to trust. Fear is an amazing thing when it's something that comes from within, not brought on by trying to fit into societal norms.

Here's what I'm fearful of: back to normal means speed, rush, multitasking, achieving, doing—not just being. That's the core of it, the concern that I will forget the gift of pause, the gift to be still and quiet in my mind. It was the reason my vision of my business was born: hoping, praying, that others would dip their toe in the still water and realize, I needed this too.

The ego will try to shame and diminish my goals. But I have to believe that a little community center that will be a constant reminder to slow down, can be a staple we need.

Taking care of yourself should be treated like a religion—we can't go long without coming together to honor the faith, honor yourself, or you'll get lost.

Don't jump off the diving board into the deep end of life's demands without your floaties!

Affirmation: *I look for signs, starting within my body, to guide me to pause.*

Lean Into Life

As life transpires, we run into obstacles we thought were only made for others: loss of loved one; broken relationships; facing sickness; loneliness; depression; anxiety; lack of connection; chronic stress; insomnia; or simply seeking a deeper understanding of your purpose in life. I call them *obstacles* because each feeling, stage, experience, can make us feel stuck.

I ask myself: am I running on empty, spinning every day without any time out? Do I take care of everyone else first before myself?

I had my share of these so-called obstacles and spent much of my time trying to embrace myself fully and move through. It's been quite a journey so far, but something happened when I lit a new fire. It didn't matter that I thought I'd spent over ten years working through these obstacles, I was still feeling stuck.

When I opened my heart and soul, it lit a fire to ignite my soul's purpose on this planet. I believed God gave me two children with special needs because I was the right parent for them, and that was my purpose. As time went on, I started to feel like I was failing at the purpose big time. My unattainable expectation of the type of mother I should be was tearing me apart. Through many years of therapy and self-reflection, it seemed my purpose needed to start *for me*—and then it would spread through to others.

I manifested the idea of Just Be through my own journey for growth and wellness. I experienced a glimpse of a life, over one weekend, where time seemed to stand still and the universe allowed me to look within. I was granted a pause, to just be, and my body literally revolted (with a trip to the ER) when I tried to go back to my everyday grind. I was smacked with the realization that I had been depleted for many years, and although I had tried to exercise, meditate, have times with friends, all I was doing was maintaining my level of drowning. I'd gotten *very* used to being underwater.

My body and soul demanded I take a break. My mind resisted. Then, once my mind caught on, all I could think was why does it have to take going away to grant us time to just be? How can I create a safe-haven for people to give back to themselves? The inspiration for *Just Be— Personalized Wellness Retreat* to administer the Just Be Journey was born.

Opening *Just Be* will grow the population of people who truly take time for themselves which will ultimately reduce our epidemic of chronic stress on a local and then global level, where compassion will grow.

Find what ignites you and LEAN INTO LIFE.

Journal Exercises: Awakening

As I mentioned in the beginning, the awakening is hard, painful, slow, but I believe, so completely necessary.

Use these challenging journal exercises to ignite a fire of awakening within you.

1. What line are you 'marching' within? What would happen if you hit the pause button? (Ref: Building in a Pause; Morning Mantra).
2. Joy and wholeness are waiting for you! How will you grab hold of it through self-care? What is your 'on break' sign? How will you stand firm to keep others from taking it down? (Ref: On Break; Get the "Should" Out of Here!).
3. Reflect on a time in your life when you might have given yourself completely to someone else (e.g., child, spouse, parent, friend) and forgot to take care of yourself. Write down all the emotions that rise. (Ref: Take Care; People Pleaser).
4. Imagine Lady Justice—in your life what is she holding in each scale? What is she trying to balance for you? What do you think it means? (Ref: Balancing Scales).
5. If you are looking in the mirror, what do you see? What do you think others would say? Is it different? Why? What would it take to be the same person? (Ref: Self-Aware; Like an Angel).
6. Are you ready to wake up? What aspect do you yearn to change and what are you holding tightly onto? What is it you need? Start there. (Ref: Lean Into Life; Diving Board).

Final Thoughts from Liz

Are You Ready to Just Be?

Pens and pencils down, time's up. For now, my story is told, although, this won't be the last you hear of me. Now it's your time. Your time to discover, uncover, investigate, sit, breathe, pause, and JUST BE. If you haven't already, you'll see what amazing light can happen when you stop chasing, racing, 'should-ing' yourself all over the place. I can't wait to hear all about it. I know for me, my healing will be ever-evolving, but today, I can TRUST in my knowing, my learning, and be brave to share it.

Everything I learned was already within me. That's the ultimate beauty of all of this—you have it inside; it's already there! Your light is bright, you might just need to find your switch to turn it on, and keep it on. Don't let the fear of what mess your light will shine deter you— *embrace your mess*. It's one of the amazing connections we have with each other—the messiness. You can do this; you can sit in your mess and shine eternal.

I believe in you, do you?

To reach out to me visit: www.justbethejourney.com/book

Acknowledgements

I must first acknowledge the powerful women in my life who have never left my side. The strength that comes from a sisterhood is unsurpassed. Without all the individual names, I thank my childhood crew for always holding me in their hearts as one of their own. I thank my local crew, who although individually unique, provide the daily shoulder and ear that is so needed. And most importantly I thank my mother and grandmothers. Readers of this book might draw an incorrect conclusion of my relationship with my bloodline—the deepest truth is I am everything I have become today because of them.

Also, much of my journey could not have happened if it wasn't for my therapist, Dr. Cynthia Nye. Always professional, she managed to guide me in the most intimate way towards loving myself unconditionally. She modeled the way and for that I am eternally grateful.

It's my hope that although this journey was deep in female strength, much can be attained for anyone. I thank my children's father for being who I needed him to be to learn the lessons I needed to learn. I honor my children for all they teach me each day. Lastly, I thank my hubby for honoring my strength and joining me on my journey.

My hope is that when the time is right, this book will find you.

About the Author

Liz Kametz is an author, coach, business owner, and most importantly, a mom of four children (two special needs, two step-children), one anxious rescue dog, and a wife to a loving hubby, who together share in our journey of learning and growth.

Professionally, she's earned degrees in Chemical Engineering, Systems Engineering, and is Six Sigma and Change Management Certified. She has twisted and turned through corporate America, hospitality and entrepreneurship, with over twenty years of experience in overcoming and trouble-shooting systemic problems in business and how to create new methods through human nature and self-growth.

The birth of *Just Be—Personalized Self-Care Retreat* came from a recognition of her own deficient self-care through the epidemic of chronic stress as a result of overwork and a need for perfection. She's able to use her first-hand experience to address the needs of others in order to guide them in creating much-needed 'pauses' each and every day, like mini-retreats, that bring in balance on a day-to-day basis, rather than waiting for a once-a-year vacation that is quickly short-lived.

As a compassionate problem-solver, she is providing solutions to help others to solve the chronic stress epidemic by supporting people. Those who are seeking the most efficient and effective way to restore their wellness and find the benefit of unique healing services, will benefit with working with her, and most importantly, connecting with a compassionate community.

About the Cover Design

Liz Kametz and business partner, Adrienne Gervais, asked all their close friends and family to provide one word that describes them. Liz had a vision of placing these words on wood – 'Wood with Meaning' – and place them as a foundation to the reception desk at *Just Be— Personalized Self-Care Retreat,* as a representation that we are never alone and *always* supported. The cover design by John Mik of Mik Advertising & Design, LLC utilized imagery from this reception desk.

Best Laid Plans—
Just Be®: A Personalized Self-Care Retreat

The plan was to open an oasis like none other in my hometown in Connecticut. You can call it a day spa, but it was always planned to be more than that. The plan was to provide experiences completely unique to address many of the common ailments that come with stress. It needed to be community-focused and connect with each client in a very authentic, human way.

Then COVID-19 hit. Best laid plans, right? Or was it fate? The vision of owner and general manager, Liz and Adrienne, was put to the test as they learned about the statewide shutdown, right when they were supposed to open in April 2020.

The vision of Just Be was manifested early in 2019 when the owner Liz was running herself to the ground juggling an important full-time corporate job and managing all that comes with school-age special needs children. She found herself taking less and less time for her own self-care. Her story is not unique, in many ways we can all relate to the symptoms of chronic stress. What it might lead to, may be different. For some it's anxiety, depression, insomnia, obesity, joint pain, chronic inflammation, and the list goes on.

We understand how stress can wreak havoc both mentally and physically. Liz crafted a solution: a personalized self-care retreat, right in our own backyard, where we can take a moment to pause and *Just Be.*

Although they were not able to open in April, they continued to work diligently on their business model to ensure the right formula to approach this new norm.

The original plan included many more hands-on services like having staff of licensed massage therapists, but Liz and Adrienne knew they needed to focus on those services they had that were more self-service in nature like the foot infusion soaks and the crystal amethyst BioMat. They spent many conversations talking about the balance between 'mainstream' spa treatments and 'alternative' methods for healing. They landed on a sweet-spot with spa services safe for clients now—waxing, relaxation treatments, brow and lash tints, hoping that would grow as protocols were lifted, and the unique alternative healing modalities mentioned already as well as integrated energy work and neurofeedback therapy.

The strong business model of diversification is one the owner Liz knows well, so even opening treatment rooms to already established wellness practitioners is part of the plan. At Just Be, they want to create a community of people, clients and providers, all collaborating and working together towards the ultimate goal of healing and self-growth.

In August of 2020, in the heat of summer, and for some, in the heat of stress, so many *what-ifs* were running through our heads. What if my kids don't go back to school? or "What if I never get to work in my office again" or "What if the funding dries up and I still don't have a job?" The questions are endless and the stress is real. Now, more than ever, we need a place to Just Be, to decompress, release those worries and refresh our spirits. Liz and Adrienne have put all their ingenuity to work to stay flexible and ride this COVID-19 storm, staying true to their ultimate mission of helping people alleviate their stress.

In a world of caution and skepticism, how can anyone feel safe to go out and get pampered? Here's where we hope Just Be will weather the storm.
- Over 3000-square feet of space to help a handful of clients at a time.
- Highest standards of sanitation and safety with germ guardians in each treatment room and rigorous cleaning protocols.

- A place to be taken care of, let your stress go, either through a guided meditation during your infusion foot soak and tea ceremony, or with an independent reflection room set up with the crystal amethyst BioMat to alleviate your nerves and reduce pain from inflammation.
- Innovative workshops to help the community connect in a safe way.
- 'Just Be Kids' supplemental program for school age children to have a place for kids to be kids, to connect, play, and let their creativity grow.

The women running Just Be know what it's like to live with the chronic stress many of us are facing. They have been able to polish a diamond out of COVID-19 coal with their ideas at Just Be. To help others to focus on their own self-care so we can all continue to forge through thick and thin.

The bottom line: We all live with stress, maybe now more than ever, we could all use some help alleviating that stress, and this new oasis on the East Hartford/Glastonbury line will give all of us the chance to take a break and Just Be.

To Learn more about the author and the vision for Just Be Self-Care Retreat: justbethejourney.com/our-story

For Just Be Merchandise: justbethejourney.com/shop

For Just Be Workshops: justbethejourney.com/workshops-events

JUST BE YOU!
WORKSHOP SERIES
$60* FOR 6-WEEK ONLINE PROGRAM (REG: $120)

With:
Author Liz Kametz, MS &
Adrienne Gervais, MA
Based on Book:
Just Be: My Healing Journey to
Embrace the Mess

Are You Ready to Be Your
True Authentic You?

To Find Peace & Calm
Among the Chaos?

WEEK 1: Series Kickoff - Introductions, Virtual Vision Board

WEEK 2: The Beginnings: Understanding internal scripts and triggers

WEEK 3&4: Unlearning - Digging deep to align to the true you

WEEK 5: Self-Care - What promise can you make to yourself

WEEK 6: Letting Go to Find Our Gratitude

The Just Be You Workshop Series is a live online community experience where author Liz Kametz & business partner and Integrated Energy Therapist, Adrienne Gervais, will help guide you through a journey of self-discovery. If you've been looking for ways to make a **positive shift,** feel less alone, **uncover your truths**, this is the series for you!

SERIES INCLUDES:
(1) Signed Copy of the Book ($20 Value)
(2) Just Be Digital Workbook & Cork-Covered Journal ($20 Value)
(3) Access to Private Facebook Community with rotating newsletters & 1:1 Coaching opportunities ($500 Value)
(4) Weekly workshops with materials ($90 Value)

Register: https://www.justbethejourney.com/bookings-checkout/just-be-you-workshop-series

*Debut Pricing, Limited Time Offer

Made in USA - North Chelmsford, MA
1174739_9781735716602
10.06.2020 0837